NO LONGER PROPERTY
OF ANYTHINK
RANGEVIEW LIBRARY
DISTRICT

D0950068

Kindness
and
Wonder

ALSO BY GAVIN EDWARDS

The World According to Tom Hanks:
The Life, the Obsessions, the Good Deeds of
America's Most Decent Guy

The Beautiful Book of Exquisite Corpses:
A Creative Game of Limitless Possibilities (editor)

The Tao of Bill Murray:
Real-Life Stories of Joy, Enlightenment,
and Party Crashing

Can I Say: Living Large, Cheating Death,
and Drums, Drums, Drums (with Travis Barker)

Last Night at the Viper Room:
River Phoenix and the Hollywood He Left Behind

VJ: The Unplugged Adventures of MTV's First Wave
(with Nina Blackwood, Mark Goodman,
Alan Hunter, and Martha Quinn)

Is Tiny Dancer Really Elton's Little John?:
Music's Most Enduring Mysteries,
Myths, and Rumors Revealed

'Scuse Me While I Kiss this Guy:
And Other Misheard Lyrics

Kindness
and
Wonder

Why Mister Rogers

Matters Now

More Than Ever

GAVIN EDWARDS

Illustrations by R. Sikoryak

DEY ST.

An Imprint of WILLIAM MORROW

KINDNESS AND WONDER. Copyright © 2019 by Gavin Edwards. Illustrations copyright © 2019 by R. Sikoryak. All rights reserved. Printed in the United States of America. No part of this book may be used or reproduced in any manner whatsoever without written permission except in the case of brief quotations embodied in critical articles and reviews. For information, address HarperCollins Publishers, 195 Broadway, New York, NY 10007.

HarperCollins books may be purchased for educational, business, or sales promotional use. For information, please email the Special Markets Department at SPsales@harpercollins .com.

FIRST EDITION

Designed by Paula Russell Szafranski

Library of Congress Cataloging-in-Publication Data has been applied for.

ISBN 978-0-06-295074-1

19 20 21 22 23   DIX/LSC   10 9 8 7 6 5 4 3 2 1

For Dashiell and Strummer,
who make every day special

Contents

Introduction:
Hello, Neighbor

It's not your imagination. Way too many people are working overtime to make our world a worse place to live: meaner, louder, dumber, crasser, more selfish. Maybe that's because Mister Rogers isn't around anymore. When he was alive, Fred Rogers stood stalwart against humanity's nastiest impulses, doing everything he could to make the world a better place. That made him a hero, but he wanted you to know he wasn't the only one.

So before he died in 2003, he offered a piece of advice that people seem to revisit every time there's a natural disaster or a mass murder—in other words, way too often these days. It's not just comforting, it's honest and it has enduring value—like Fred Rogers himself.

Mister Rogers confided, "My mother used to say, a long time ago, whenever there would be any real catastrophe . . . she would say, 'Always look for the helpers. There will always be helpers—just on the sidelines.' That's why I think if news programs could make a conscious effort of showing rescue teams, of showing medical people—anybody who is coming into a place where there's a tragedy, to be sure that they include that. Because if you look for the helpers, you'll know that there's hope."

In a few sentences, Mister Rogers not only offered solace: he helped turn despair into action. Somebody who sees that there are helpers in the world's worst hours, and that they make a difference, is somebody who stops watching and starts helping. Mister Rogers did all that in a slow and even voice, because that was how he talked. It was easier for children to understand him on his TV program *Mister Rogers' Neighborhood* if he spoke slowly, and he didn't care if adults found it laughable. He was comfortable measuring his words, so he said what he meant, and he was even more comfortable with silence, so he could listen and think.

From a distance, it looked like Mister Rogers was stuck in first gear, but he actually operated with very few wasted moments and words: that high degree of efficiency was part of the reason he accomplished so much in his life.

AS A CHILD IN THE EARLY 1970S, I WATCHED *MISTER ROGERS' Neighborhood* faithfully every afternoon. Our TV set was black-and-white while our couch was a lurid green, but the monochromatic world of the *Neighborhood* seemed just as vivid as my own life. My favorite part of the show was the Neighborhood of Make-Believe, filled with fantastic beings like X the Owl and Henrietta Pussycat. I had no idea that Fred Rogers was manipulating those puppets—I thought of him as the kind man who knew the way to Make-Believe and kept telling me that he liked me just the way I was.

I needed to hear that. I was an awkward and lonely child,

made entirely of elbows and stubbed toes, but when I watched *Mister Rogers' Neighborhood,* I felt calmer, as if the world I was making for myself would be exactly as large as I needed it to be.

The years passed, and I moved on to other television programming, first *Batman* and *The Brady Bunch,* and later MTV and *Twin Peaks.* As I got older, I would occasionally catch a glimpse of my other childhood favorite, *Sesame Street,* and reliably enjoy Muppets doing song parodies ("Rebel L"!) or Cookie Monster acting as a furry blue id. But *Mister Rogers' Neighborhood* made no particular effort to entertain adults who happened to be watching: Fred Rogers only wanted to take care of the nation's children, a half hour at a time, for as long as they needed him. That devotion was manifest in every sentence he spoke, enunciating each syllable with care, measuring out lessons about how the world worked, everywhere from the crayon factory to the sandbox.

I took what I needed from the show, and then I forgot about what Mister Rogers had done for me. In college, I even put together a prank, one in a series where friends and I made flyers for fictional events like the deliberately incoherent "Rally for Change." This one was a memorial candlelight vigil for Fred Rogers—who wasn't dead, but who seemed irrelevant to my life as a nineteen-year-old. A few people believed the flyers and showed up; everybody said nice things about what Mister Rogers meant to them, so somehow his sincerity triumphed, even after being forced through the snarky apparatus that was my sense of humor circa 1990. (The campus learned what had happened, so a few weeks later, we faked them out with a similar memorial service for Alan Hale Jr., who had played the Skipper on *Gilligan's Island*—but who surprised everyone by actually being dead.)

A few years later, I was working in New York City as a junior editor and staff writer at *Details,* the glossy magazine that Condé Nast had positioned as the hip kid brother of *GQ.* One day, I got a surprising phone call: a publicist pitching an interview with Fred Rogers. The PR man was David Newell, who didn't mention that he was also the actor who played Mr. McFeely of the Speedy Delivery Service on the *Neighborhood.*

I suggested that Mister Rogers would be a good candidate for our back-page interview series called "Rites of Passage," which I had recently inaugurated with a Q&A with Steven Tyler of Aerosmith. Newell blanched at some of the racier questions, and even after I offered to steer around any porn-related queries, he politely declined on his boss's behalf.

That would have been a forgettably routine interaction—the magazine articles that get printed are dwarfed by the ones that never quite come together—except that a year later, Tom Junod wrote a cover story for *Esquire* in which he spent extensive time with Fred Rogers and elegantly portrayed his humanity and his legacy. (It's the article that inspired the 2019 Tom Hanks movie *It's a Beautiful Day in the Neighborhood.*)

I had remembered Mister Rogers only as a benign, upright figure from my childhood—iconic enough that I was happy to talk to him but not important enough that I would insist on it. Until I read Junod's article, I had no idea of his utter sincerity and his singular devotion to children—and I had forgotten how much he had helped me. So I missed the story and I never got to thank Mister Rogers personally—but he didn't need my gratitude. His life's work was helping children, and it didn't matter whether you thanked him. It didn't even matter whether you remembered him when you grew up. He was going to keep doing his job every day anyway: awakening the imaginations of children and treating them with kindness served as reward enough.

ASKED IN 1983 TO EXPLAIN WHO HE WAS, MISTER ROGERS BEGAN, as he so often did, with music. "I'm a composer and a piano player," he said, "a writer and a television producer, almost by accident a performer, a husband and a father. And I'm a minister. You know, most of us are many things, and I remember the marvelous feeling I had when I realized that many parts of who I am could be brought together to work for children and their families. That's what I am the most: a man who cares deeply about children."

What do you call a man like that? For millions of children who watched him on public television over five decades, he was simply Mister Rogers, the man who told them that he liked them just the way they were. While "Mister Rogers" wasn't a character that Fred Rogers adopted for the camera—what you see is what you get, the people who knew him best often said—it was his public face, with contact lenses and prewritten dialogue. While the sweaters he wore on the show were his own, away from the studio he would often be found in a turtleneck or a three-piece suit. Off camera, he encouraged people, especially his friends, to call him Fred. In this book, I will call him both "Mister Rogers" and "Fred," depending on context—and if the latter seems shockingly informal to you, I will remind you that Fred thought of you as his friend.

Amazingly, Mister Rogers' litany of his skills and accomplishments left out some major boldface sections of his résumé. He was a puppeteer who manipulated most of the major puppet characters on *Mister Rogers' Neighborhood,* lurking behind the scenery for segments in the Neighborhood of Make-Believe. He was a writer who penned most of the episodes of the *Neighborhood* longhand on legal pads (and edited the ones he didn't write).

Fred Rogers had an old-fashioned patina when he was

alive, as if he belonged in a lineup next to sepia-toned Civil War chess set salesmen. Even though his philosophy on child development was modern to the point of being cutting-edge, what people remember best is his slow-paced cadence, which seemed to belong to a time before email and text messages. Programming for a world that has its finger on the fast-forward button, PBS has since rotated *Mister Rogers' Neighborhood* off its airwaves in favor of the cartoon *Daniel Tiger's Neighborhood.*

When I showed my own children episodes of *Mister Rogers' Neighborhood,* they watched them tolerantly enough and pronounced them "sweet," but it was clear they didn't connect with the show the way they did with *Teen Titans Go!* or Dude Perfect videos on YouTube. I tried to remember that they're not required to love everything that mattered to me as a child, even though this show would likely have been good for their souls. I may have introduced it to them too late—as in every generation, kids today seem to grow up faster than ever.

If most children today aren't watching *Mister Rogers' Neighborhood*—and they aren't—then what position does Mister Rogers occupy in the cultural firmament of the twenty-first century? Is he just a figure of nostalgia, a genius who's fondly remembered but mostly unwatched, like Buster Keaton? Well, honestly, yes—he'll never again have the impact on the world (especially the USA) that he did circa 1974. But "nostalgia" is just another way to spell "cultural legacy." At the moment you are reading this book, Mister Rogers has enough purchase on your heart to change the society that you live in.

While working on this book, I watched countless episodes of the *Neighborhood*. It reminded me of days on the bright green couch, but it wasn't a magical time machine that returned me to the innocence of youth: I was an adult watching a show made for children. These episodes didn't blot out the stresses of adulthood or the horrors of the modern world—but they did calm me and bring me a sense of purpose. Every morning I spent watching the show strengthened my core: not my abdominal muscles, but my emotional well-being.

I recommend the experience: *Mister Rogers' Neighborhood* is easily found on DVD or streaming video, and can provide balm in these troubled times. But you don't need to binge-watch the series to renew yourself, because if you ever spent time with the show, you carry the Neighborhood wherever you go.

"The child is father of the man," William Wordsworth wrote in his 1802 poem "My Heart Leaps Up." Fred Rogers would have revised the language to be more gender-inclusive, but he would have approved of the sentiment. Our childhood experiences form our mature selves, which is why he worked so tirelessly to enrich the lives of children—and why adults have access to the wisdom and miracles of their own childhood. A rainbow seems like a polychromatic miracle at any age, even if as an adult you know you can find one as close as the nearest lawn sprinkler. And when you're grown up, you remember what Mister Rogers taught you, even if you don't remember that the lesson came from him.

In any era, Mister Rogers is a curative voice for all people who choose to listen, but when the world is especially fraught, as it is now, he becomes even more crucial. His ability to build his legacy is just as important as the specifics of his message: it reminds all of us that good works don't evaporate, but shape the memories and lives of the people around us. That's why the first half of this book, "Let's Make the Most of This Beautiful Day," tells the story of Fred Rogers' remarkable life. By looking squarely at how he spent his seventy-four years on this planet, you will be better equipped to build a lasting legacy of your own, whether its positive effects ripple across the world or remain confined to your own neighborhood.

The second half of this book, "Ten Ways to Live More Like Mister Rogers Right Now," distills his wisdom and his daily actions into specific precepts. If you choose, you can emulate his life and find ways to be one of society's helpers. That doesn't necessarily mean becoming an emergency medical technician or rushing into a burning building to save lives. But since the world is on fire—which, given the rapid pace of climate change, has changed from a vivid metaphor to the literal truth in a shockingly short period of time—we all need to be helpers.

I don't need to itemize the world's current ills: the hatred, the cruelty, the resurgence of fascism, the children in cages, the squandering of our future for profit. The specific headlines change at an overwhelming speed, and negativity and hatred and ignorance all reinforce each other. It's completely understandable if, in the face of constant disaster and atrocities, your impulse is to hide under the covers.

You should know, however, that Mister Rogers wouldn't want you to give in to despair—it's not good for the world, and it's not good for you. He believed that by talking about our greatest fears and trials, we could conquer them, both in our hearts and in the world. Changing people's attitudes is the only way to achieve mass action—which is what we need to save our planet.

Consider, for a moment, climate change. The polar ice is melting and the United Nations estimates that one million different animal species are at risk of extinction. But although humanity has badly fouled its own nest, there's still a wide range of possible outcomes: an average rise of two degrees Celsius (from preindustrial global temperatures) would mean more disasters and famine, but a rise of four degrees would probably mean worldwide ecological and societal collapse. Every half degree of heat in that range could mean millions of lives, and so every half degree is vitally important, even if the coral reefs prove to be a lost cause. When firefighters can't rescue everyone from a burning building, they still save as many lives as they can. A better world is worth fighting for.

Fred Rogers was the gentlest of men—but he was also a fighter. His chosen weapons were puppets and scripts and songs, but he battled every day to improve the world he lived in. He focused particularly on children, because they needed the most help, but he also knew that winning their hearts and minds would help tilt the planet onto a better axis, many years after they stopped watching his show.

We can be like Mister Rogers. We too can make the world a better place, with love and forgiveness and kindness and wonder.

PART I

Let's Make the Most of This Beautiful Day

FRED ROGERS ENTERED THE WORLD WITH A SERIOUS DISADVAN-
tage, albeit a typical one: he was born a child. Many people
leave behind the confusion and fear of their earliest years as
quickly as possible, so that by the time they're old enough to
vote, their own childhoods seem like half-forgotten television
shows starring somebody else. Fred Rogers never forgot how
powerless and disoriented he felt when he was young, and he
made it his life's work to help any children who were also on
that hard road—which is to say, all of them.

Fred McFeely Rogers was born on March 20, 1928, in his
grandparents' stately brick house in Latrobe, Pennsylvania.
Latrobe was a prosperous town roughly forty miles east of
Pittsburgh—connected to the larger city by the Main Line of
the Pennsylvania Railroad, which ran through the middle of
town. (Latrobe later became famous as the home of Rolling
Rock; the beer was first sold in 1939.) When Fred was a kid,
the town's population was 11,111: "I was thrilled with all those
ones," Fred remembered.

The McFeelys weren't plutocrats on the scale of the Mellons or the Heinzes—the leading dynasties of the industrial behemoth that was Pittsburgh—but Fred was born into one of the most prominent families in Latrobe. His father, James Hillis Rogers, had worked at the McFeely Brick Company (which manufactured the silica bricks that lined steel furnaces) and, as Fred put it years later, "married the boss's daughter," Nancy McFeely Rogers. Jim Rogers went on to be president of that company and other industrial firms such as Latrobe Die Casting, eventually running a bank. Fred was born on the eve of the Great Depression, but his family never stood in bread lines.

Fred's family lived in a three-story mansion on the same block as his grandparents, in the prosperous section of Latrobe called "The Hill." (The type of neighborhood Woody Guthrie wrote bitter working-class anthems about, basically.) The household staff included a cook, a chauffeur, and a nanny for young Fred. That nanny, Ella Jane Dinco, started working for the family when she was eighteen years old and Fred was a newborn; she stayed for eight years. She so admired Nancy Rogers that when her own daughter was born she named *her* Nancy as well. "Mrs. Rogers was like my mom's mother," said that girl, who grew up to be Nancy Donahue. "She took care of her always."

As a young girl, Donahue often accompanied her mother when she went to work at the Rogers home. She vividly remembered one day when she was in the kitchen, hiding under a big table and sobbing, because she had just had a traumatic visit to the dentist. The teenage Fred Rogers got down on the kitchen floor and comforted her.

Jim Rogers, by all accounts, was a benevolent boss, genuinely caring about the lives of his workers—if he heard they had hard times at home, he would do what he could to help with loans or discreet gifts. (When he died, there were thousands of small loans on the company books, money extended to its employees that he had never had the heart to collect.)

Similarly, Nancy Rogers spent most of her time on various philanthropic efforts, organizing a consortium of local churches to help families in need and volunteering at the Latrobe Hospital. (As a teenager, she had lied about her age to get a driver's license so she could haul bandages and medical supplies during the flu epidemic of 1918. She had aspired to be a doctor, but the cultural norms of that era made that impossible.) Nancy Rogers set an excellent example of giving to others while doting on her son: he grew up knowing he was loved. But under his mother's unblinking eye, he also grew up anxious and cosseted.

In 1932, Charles Lindbergh, a pilot who had become one of the most famous men in the United States by making the first solo flight across the Atlantic Ocean, became the center of a blockbuster news story: his twenty-month-old son, Charles Lindbergh Jr., was kidnapped from his own nursery, held for fifty thousand dollars' ransom, and eventually found dead with a crushed skull.

The Rogers family had been overprotective before, but now, fearing that their wealth would make them an attractive target for a kidnapper, they went on high alert. Fred wasn't allowed to leave the house to play outside unless he notified an adult and was supervised. When Fred went to the Second Ward elementary school, a chauffeur would not only drop him off and bring him home at the end of the day, he would take him and a playmate home at midday. After they ate a lunch prepared by the family cook, the children would head upstairs to the attic that had been refurbished as a playroom, complete with a puppet theater stage where Fred liked to put on shows.

That playmate, Peggy Moberg McFeaters, remembered, "Fred had more of everything than I did—especially toys. Soldiers, castles, forts, and things like that." They would spread them out on the floor and play with them until returning to school—or on weekend visits, for hours. McFeaters said, "Fred was always so imaginative. Looking back on it, I sometimes think it was Mister Rogers' Neighborhood and he was showing me around." But he wasn't used to having a playmate his own age, she said. "The thing that always struck me was how he used to look at me. It was more like he was watching me play than he was playing himself."

"I had every childhood disease that came down the pike," Fred later said. "Even scarlet fever." One of Fred's ailments was asthma—exacerbated by all the heavy manufacturing in Latrobe, which was in the middle of Pennsylvania coal country—and so he was often kept inside, not just to foil kidnappers, but so that he might benefit from the family's expensive new air conditioner. Even as a child, he understood his family's privileged position in Latrobe and took pride in their charity, but he also knew that the family money set him apart.

"Fred was the richest kid in town," said his classmate Richard Jim. The extravagant luxury that particularly impressed Jim: Fred owned seven different pairs of corduroy pants.

If Fred ever forgot that he didn't fit in, the other kids at school were all too happy to remind him. He was relentlessly teased and tormented. Fred was pale, asthmatic, chubby, squeaky-voiced, clumsy, shy, and rich. He was also kind and funny and bright, but nobody seemed to notice that.

Living near the Rogers family was an elderly woman named Mama Bell Frampton. Whenever Fred wanted a snack, or just some company, he knew Mama Bell would welcome him into her kitchen. "She loved children," he said. "Every time I needed a treat, I'd knock on her back door and she'd welcome me. 'Come for toast sticks, Freddy?' She knew me well."

The recipe for "toast sticks" was simple: toast with butter and jam, cut into slices. It was nevertheless a banner day when Mama Bell asked Fred if he wanted to learn how to make them. He was five or six, but he vividly remembered it decades later: "She let me put the bread in the toaster and the butter and jam on the toast, and she even let me (ever so carefully) cut the toast into four long 'sticks.'" He was proud of the sticks and that Mama Bell had trusted him to make them: "I often think of Mama Bell because I think she really did love me. She just somehow sensed what I needed in order to grow."

One afternoon, Fred's school let out early. The chauffeur wasn't aware of the modified schedule, so he wasn't waiting at the curb as per usual. Young Fred, feeling mature and responsible, decided to walk the ten blocks home himself. He wasn't abducted by any kidnappers—but he did attract the attention of some of his schoolmates. "It wasn't long before I sensed I was being followed by a whole group of boys," he said. He picked up his pace, but they stayed with him: "As I walked faster, I looked around. They called my name and came closer and closer, and got louder and louder."

He ran, with a gang of bullies in hot pursuit, calling, "Freddy, hey, fat Freddy! We're going to get you, Freddy."

Fred took shelter at a nearby house and eventually made it back home. In his second-floor bedroom, with the yellow wallpaper that had scenes of Parisian life, he was safe. That didn't mean he was happy there, or even comfortable. He said, "I was used to neat-as-a-pin parlors with porcelain figures that seemed to whisper 'Not to be touched!'—to clean, starched shirts and neatly combed hair warning 'Not to be mussed!'—and to the inevitable wagging of an adult's 'Don't you do that, you might hurt yourself!' finger."

The turning point, when the porcelain figure escaped from its box, came when Fred was eight years old. His mother's parents, the McFeelys, had a home around the corner from the Rogers house in Latrobe, another in the tony Squirrel Hill neighborhood of Pittsburgh, and a family farm called Buttermilk Falls, where a rustic house and a redbrick barn were surrounded by acres of land, crisscrossed by old stone walls. Fred spent many Sunday afternoons on his grandparents' farm, wandering the property, checking on the cows and pigs, and looking longingly at the dilapidated walls—they were missing stones in some places, and actively crumbling in others. Fred longed to climb those walls and explore them, but wouldn't dream of doing it without permission.

So one afternoon, after Sunday dinner, he shyly came into the drawing room where the adults had gathered for tea and coffee and conversation. Summoning every ounce of courage in his body, Fred cleared his throat.

Nobody noticed.

"Hey," Fred said quietly, but just loud enough for the adults to pay attention. "I, uh, I want to climb the stone walls. Can I climb the stone walls?"

As Fred remembered it, "instantly a chorus went up from the women in the room"—led by his mother.

"Heavens, no!" they told him. "You'll hurt yourself!"

That was the reaction that Fred expected—so predictable that he wasn't even disappointed. But then his grandfather's voice boomed through the drawing room. "Now hold on just a minute," Grandfather McFeely said. "So the boy wants to climb the walls. *Then let the boy climb the walls!* He has to learn to do things for himself."

Fred went outside before anybody could change their minds. "For the next two and a half hours, I climbed those old walls—skinned my knee, tore my pants, and had the time of my life," he said.

When he was done, he found his grandfather and told him all about his glorious life-threatening adventures. Grandfather McFeely had something important to say to his grandson: "Fred, you made this day a special day, just by being yourself. Always remember, there's just one person in this whole world like you—and I like you just the way you are."

A valuable message for any child to hear—but exactly the words of unconditional love and approval that anxious eight-year-old Fred needed. It cemented the bond between Fred McFeely Rogers and Fred Brooks McFeely. The boy called his beloved grandfather "Ding-Dong," because when he was very young he had sat on his lap and learned the nursery rhyme "Ding Dong Dell." ("Ding dong dell / Pussy's in the well.")

Fred was also close with his maternal grandmother, Nancy McFeely, who he called "Nana"; she took a particular interest in his musical ability. Fred's parents bought him a small pump organ for twenty-five dollars (the equivalent of five hundred dollars today) and he proved to be a quick pupil, impressing his family with his ability to hear a song once and then play it by ear.

"I was always able to cry or laugh or say I was angry through the tips of my fingers on the piano. I would go to the piano even when I was five years old, and start to play how I felt," Fred said. "In those days, you didn't speak your feelings as much as express them artistically."

When Fred was ten, he told Nana how much he longed for a piano of his own. Fred, who didn't typically wheedle her for expensive gifts, earnestly explained that to grow as a pianist, he needed a better instrument. Nana indulgently told him that if he picked out a piano, she would pay for it, figuring that it couldn't cost that much. The next time Fred was visiting the McFeelys at their Pittsburgh home, he announced that he wanted to go shopping for his piano. Nana gave him directions to the Steinway & Sons showroom and he rode the trolley four miles.

For hours, he worked his way through the store, playing on every piano they had available, before deciding which one he liked best: a Steinway Concert Grand Model D, a half-ton top-of-the-line model that might be found in concert halls. (Fred had a good ear.) Made in 1920, it was in extraordinary condition, having recently received an "heirloom" renovation in New York.

Fred solemnly announced that he wanted to buy the grand piano, and the salesmen quietly snickered: it cost almost three thousand dollars (about seventy thousand dollars today), clearly not affordable for a child, no matter how lucrative his paper route. It was a choice made by a young man who had never worried about money. But Nana kept her promise and Fred soon returned to the Steinway showroom, armed with a check for the full cost of the piano. He kept that piano for the rest of his life: it set his life on a trajectory through the world of music and the arts, and he used it to compose hundreds of songs, including his most famous tunes.

As an adult, still grateful for the gift from Nana that changed his life, Fred said simply, "There's something very mystical and wonderful about how music can touch us. It's elemental."

Fred still felt like a misfit, but he was quietly turning into an overachiever: "I was trying to learn so many things at once, things like the piano and organ and algebra and cooking and typing, and I even started to take clarinet lessons." There was a hitch, though. "I just didn't practice the clarinet, so I didn't learn. I think I wanted to learn by magic. I think I had the idea that if I got the clarinet I would somehow know how to play it." The untouched clarinet remained in its case, reproaching him and reminding him that many of the skills he wanted to master would be harder to learn than making toast sticks.

Fred's parents had been warned against having any more children after Fred—Nancy might not survive another birth, the doctors told her. So Fred grew up as an only child until he was eleven, when the Rogers family adopted a six-month-old baby girl, called "Laney." Fred "was so kind and so sweet," his sister, Nancy Elaine Rogers Crozier, said as an adult. "He would carry me around. He would walk with me, hand in hand. He would follow me around the yard, so I didn't trip and fall. But I'm sure there were times when he just wished this little thing hadn't come to live in the house with him."

Laney's arrival didn't change the fundamental dynamics

of the Rogers family: Jim was loving but aloof, Nancy was loving but smothering, and Fred was loving but uncomfortable in his own skin. They attended services at the local Presbyterian church, took expensive vacations in Florida and New York City, and once in a while busted out a cupboard of musical instruments for a spontaneous, cacophonous parade through the house.

Nancy Rogers set an example of giving to others—not just through her charitable work, but with a Christmas list that had five hundred names on it. Among the bounty of gifts every year were a dozen sweaters that she hand-knitted: one for each of the twelve dearest people in her life. On Christmas Day, Nancy would take requests for the following year: she knitted one sweater a month. "I know what kind you want, Freddy," she would tell her son. "You want the one with the zipper up the front."

Fred Rogers entered Latrobe High School in the fall of 1942, while World War II raged from Stalingrad to Guadalcanal. "When I got to high school, I was scared to death to go to school. Every day, I was afraid I was going to fail," he said. "I resented those kids for not seeing beyond my fatness or my shyness. I didn't know that it was alright to resent it, to feel bad about it, even to feel very sad about it. I didn't know it was alright to feel any of those things, because the advice I got from the grown-ups was 'Just let on you don't care—then nobody will bother you.'"

Fred, however, couldn't pretend that he didn't care. His emotional honesty would be one of his great strengths as an adult, but as an adolescent, he wasn't able to be an insouciant teenager, or even to impersonate one plausibly. He favored solitary hobbies such as photography; a darkroom was duly installed in the basement of the Rogers home.

Fred decided that if he couldn't change how he felt, at least he could change how he looked. He had seen the advertisements for the Charles Atlas bodybuilding course—omnipresent in comic books and boys' magazines, they featured a "97-pound weakling" who got sand kicked in his face on the beach until he got muscular and stood up to the bullies. Fred saved up his nineteen dollars and sent away for the lessons.

"In 1944, I was a chubby and weak sixteen-year-old, and Charles Atlas was trim and strong," Fred said. "I did the exercises every morning—some of them even had me hanging on a bar at a doorjamb. Many months and many lessons later, I still didn't look like Charles Atlas." He would find his way forward not through dynamic tension and bulging muscles, but through an act of kindness, and the friendship that resulted.

"In our class there was this big man on campus by the name of Jim Stumbaugh," Fred said. Jim, popular with his classmates, was a star of the track team, the basketball team, and the football team. At a football practice, Jim sustained a serious injury to a kidney that landed him in the hospital. The Rogers family and the Stumbaugh family were friendly, so Nancy arranged for her son to bring the golden teenage god the homework he was missing, hoping that the two boys would forge a connection.

Fred and Jim were initially baffled by each other: saying they traveled in different social circles implies that Fred had a social circle. But "we started to talk, and I could see what substance there was in this jock. And evidently, he could see what substance there was in this shy kid." Fred and Jim became close friends, a bond that lasted past high school graduation, through the rest of their lives.

Fred said, "When he got out of the hospital and went back to school, he said to people, 'That Rogers kid's okay.' That made all the difference in the world to me." With his confidence boosted, Fred started writing for the paper and eventually edited the yearbook. He competed in oratorical contests, he was president of the student council, and whenever things got slow at school dances he would entertain his classmates by singing a rowdy song about the beheading of Anne Boleyn. He even had a girlfriend, Doris Stewart, the class valedictorian, whom he took to the senior prom. As an adult, Dr. Doris Pennoyer described Fred as a "very determined person. Whatever he decided to do got done."

On graduation in the spring of 1946, Fred was voted "most likely to succeed" by his classmates. Years later, he said of Jim, "What a difference one person can make in the life of others."

One year behind Fred Rogers at Latrobe High was a young man who would end up being just as famous as him: Arnold Palmer, who became the dominant golfer of his generation, winning sixty-two PGA tournaments and earning the nickname "The King." "He was a very meticulous student. He didn't run with the guys I did, and he didn't drink beer," Palmer said of Fred Rogers in 2011. "His interests were music and religion and history and that sort of thing. But a nice guy. We liked each other."

Although Rogers had once won a four-mile swimming race, nobody would ever mistake him for a jock. One time, Palmer's father—Milfred "Deacon" Palmer, the golf pro at the local country club—gave Fred a golf lesson. All parties agreed that

Fred didn't have untapped athletic talents. Fred joked of the lessons that the elder Palmer gave to Fred and Arnold, "One of us did a lot more with it than the other."

There was no second round of golf, but another set of lessons took. George Allen, a decade older than Fred, was the son of their former housekeeper—when she died, Allen was still young, so he lived in the Rogers house for many years. Allen grew up to become a jazz pianist and a flight instructor, teaching many of the famous Tuskegee Airmen at the historically black Tuskegee Institute in Alabama. But one of his early pupils was Fred Rogers; all through Fred's senior year, he visited the Latrobe airport for flying lessons with Allen in a tiny Piper Cub airplane.

"He was so enthusiastic about flying—I know that's why I wanted to learn," Fred said. "The best teacher in the world is somebody who loves what he or she does and just loves it in front of you." When Fred graduated from high school in the spring of 1946, he said, "I thought I was going to be an airline pilot." World War II had ended the year before, sparing the gentle, bookish Fred from any obligation to enlist in the armed forces. Instead, he headed for the Ivy League.

Fred had won admission to Dartmouth. While he considered a career as a pilot, and also thought about becoming a Presbyterian minister, he entered college intending to major in romance languages as a prelude to entering the diplomatic corps. Unfortunately, Fred and Dartmouth were a mismatch: he was a teetotaler and the all-male campus was famously lubricated by alcohol. (The school's location—Hanover, New Hampshire—was often referred to as "Hangover, New Hampshire.") Fred got along so poorly with his assigned football-player roommates, he moved out of his dorm and lived with his French teacher instead.

In the middle of his sophomore year, in the depths of a freezing New Hampshire winter, Fred thought about his future and decided that while he was an adroit linguist, what he actually loved was music. He went to the professor Arnold Kvam, a cellist who had just been recruited by Dartmouth to build up the school's music program. Kvam advised the eager young pianist to leave Dartmouth: "Fred, we won't have this department ready for you in the four years that you'll be here. Why don't you look at the place that I just came from?"

That was Rollins College, in Winter Park, Florida—so on his Easter vacation, Fred took a trip south to visit the campus. A group of young men and women in the music program were asked to show off the school to a prospective transfer. "We were delighted at the prospect of a 'new kid' on campus," said one of them, then known as Joanne Byrd. "One of our friends had a wonderful, roomy old car, and we all went to the train station to welcome Fred," she said. "After the tour, we took him to the music rooms, where we spent many hours of our college lives, and he immediately sat down at a piano. We loved his playing. Few of our small group could play the jazz and popular songs of the day with so much ease and grace, and he could play the classics, too. This 'new kid' really had talent!"

Fred was similarly impressed by his visit. "Dartmouth was very cold and Rollins was very warm," he said, referring both to the thermometer and the student bonhomie. "I just felt so much at home there." He promptly applied for a transfer; Rollins admitted him, granting him one year of credits for his two years at Dartmouth, and he enrolled in the fall of 1948.

Rollins lacked the prestige of Dartmouth: while it was the oldest college in Florida, it had a reputation as a country club for rich kids, complete with golf, tennis, and waterskiing. Kay Griffith, who attended Rollins at the same time as Fred, remembered, "It had six hundred students, and everyone knew everyone else. It was expensive, two thousand dollars a year to go there, which was a lot of money in 1949. It was a happy, wonderful place: beautiful Spanish architecture, sitting beside a lovely lake. Fred liked to swim, as I recall. We didn't have a pool—we just swam in the lake. There was a high diving board." But because it was Florida, students had to be cautious: "There were alligators in the lake."

Rollins was idyllic—if you were white and heterosexual. It didn't admit an African American student until 1964, and it quietly expelled students for being gay. This was sadly typical for colleges below the Mason-Dixon line in the late 1940s, which didn't make it any more admirable. There's no evidence Fred tried to change the school's policies, but he did join (and later chair) the Interfaith and Race Relations Committee, which focused on improving the lot of the local African American communities suffering from segregation. The committee raised funds for local libraries and schools; advocating for a medical clinic, Rogers wrote in one report, "Winter Park is in dire need of such a building since there is no colored doctor in town." Rogers acquiesced to the larger system of Jim Crow, both at the university and in local communities, but he also did what he could to ameliorate racism's systemic effects; even though these were half steps, they were radical in the eyes of some of his fellow students.

Finally finding a place where he felt at home, Fred became

one of the best-liked students on campus. He was known for his mischievous sense of humor: one sorority house on campus had a plaque outside reading LIFE IS FOR SERVICE. Fred made a habit of covering up the SER on the plaque so it read LIFE IS FOR VICE.

"It was not *all* fun and games for Fred—he had his struggles, as we all did," Joanne said. Even in the Florida sunshine, he remained a devoted student. "I remember his moaning and groaning to us, 'I just *know* I'm going to fail this course! Of course, we'd all get worried for him. Then he'd get an A—and we'd all get mad at him."

His French instructor, Baroness von Boecop, encouraged Fred to maintain his high academic standards—and to try acting. "I had never done anything onstage," Fred said, "but she forced me—in these little French productions." For example, he appeared in Jean Giraudoux's play *The Madwoman of Chaillot,* which had debuted in Paris only a few years earlier. Another Rollins student in the cast: Anthony Perkins, later famous as the star of Alfred Hitchcock's *Psycho.* "I don't think I ever wanted to be on the stage," Fred said. Trying it only confirmed to him that he preferred working in the background.

Meanwhile, Fred and Joanne were growing closer. Joanne was vivacious, funny, and an accomplished classical pianist. Their intimacy didn't extend much beyond holding hands—both were extremely shy—but they spent their free time together and their friends considered them to be a couple. They went to many school dances together, and at one costume party, they won first prize for their matching outfits as the popular dolls Raggedy Ann and Raggedy Andy. "The prize was a big bottle of champagne—what a gift for two teetotalers!" Joanne said. "We had great fun going from table to table and pouring it for everyone else."

Joanne was falling for this upright young man, often serious but also full of whimsy. Fred had a strong interest in young children and their education; he had spent so much of his childhood feeling isolated and fearful and had never forgotten how that felt. That gave him an immediate rapport with children, who could tell that he took their problems seriously. Fred already knew he wanted to help children, although he wasn't sure of the best way to do it; he frequently visited nursery schools to watch teachers at work with their young charges. Joanne thought that one day, he might end up running an orphanage.

Anthony Perkins, who was majoring in theater arts, sometimes would wander into the dorm room of Fred Rogers, who remembered the actor's musical ability. Fred said, "I had a piano in my room because I was a composition major, and Tony used to stop by and play every once in a while. He must have been able to play by ear."

Fred was working on some of his earliest musical compositions: "Variations on a Theme of Chopin" and "Three-Voice Fugue, for cello, viola, and violin," but also parodic lyrics for "Row, Row, Row Your Boat": "Propel, propel, propel your craft / Gently down liquid solution / Ecstatically ecstatically ecstatically ecstatically / Existence is but an illusion." And he began work on an opera, called *Josephine the Short-Neck Giraffe*, about an ungulate who yearns to have a longer neck. It was written in French, combining his two academic interests: Fred majored in musical composition and minored in French, graduating magna cum laude in 1951.

On the verge of his adult life, Fred felt like a kid on Ding-Dong's farm again. He had permission to go climb any of the stone walls; he just needed to decide which way to go. Being a diplomat and being an airline pilot were both achievable goals, and his father made it clear that he would be welcome to work at the family businesses, but Fred decided that what he wanted to do was help people—just not at an orphanage. His parents, especially his mother, had set a sterling example of giving selflessly to the community, and Fred took his Presbyterian faith seriously, so he applied to the Western Theological Seminary in Pittsburgh, where he could study to be a minister.

A few months before he received his diploma, Fred went home to Latrobe for Easter break, his seminary acceptance in hand. "I saw this new thing called television," he said. It was a diverting novelty, the way a new video game or smartphone would be in the twenty-first century, and the Rogers family had one of the first sets in Latrobe: the ten-inch black-and-white television set was kept in the family's "music room." Fred wasn't interested in hit shows such as *Arthur Godfrey's Talent Scouts* or *Texaco Star Theater*, starring Milton Berle; he turned the set on in the afternoon, curious to see what kind of programming it offered for children.

What he witnessed horrified him. "People were dressed up in some kind of costumes and they literally were *putting pies in each other's faces*," Fred said. He didn't regard this as slapstick comedy, fun if a bit messy—in his eyes, it debased the whole medium. "This is a wonderful tool for education—why is it being used this way?" Fred objected.

His parents had just come to terms with his desire to become a minister, but now he informed them that he had a new plan. "I don't think I'll go into seminary right away," he told them. "I think maybe I'll go into television."

"But you've never even seen it," they said, stunned that the gadget in the music room had upended their son's life.

"Well, I've seen enough of it," Fred said. "I'd like to try."

While this may have looked like an aimless twenty-three-year-old flailing around, uncertain what to do with his life, it was actually Fred Rogers' first act of genius. He saw a staticky broadcast that he found appalling, but he had the vision and the stubbornness to say that he could use the medium to create something far superior.

So Fred applied for jobs with the broadcast networks in New York City (there were four in 1951: ABC, CBS, NBC, and Du-Mont, which went out of business five years later). Fred's father pulled some strings—a friend of his was an executive at RCA, which owned NBC—and Fred got an entry-level job at the NBC Opera Theatre, the network's in-house opera company.

Fred found a one-bedroom apartment on the Upper East Side of Manhattan; his family had his Steinway grand piano hoisted out of the house and shipped to New York City. Meanwhile, Joanne was studying for her master's degree in music at Florida State University; she and Fred traded a few phone calls and letters but, uncertain whether they had a future together, fitfully dated other people.

Fred was assigned to be an assistant to the director Kirk Browning, who was just seven years older than him but already an old hand at NBC, where everybody was making up the rules of the television industry as they went along. Browning said, "I remember a very soft-spoken, sort of deferential, very appealing young man with a wry sense of humor. I do remem-

ber that he was a much better pianist at this point than I was."
When Browning discovered how beautifully Fred could render
a particular Rachmaninoff prelude, he regularly asked him to
play it.

Outside his Rachmaninoff duties, Fred was principally a
gofer, getting coffees and Cokes for the office staff and visiting
talent. He said that the experience taught him a lot about human behavior: he never forgot the day when he brought somebody a coffee and was rewarded with a withering *"I wanted milk
and not sugar."*

"I just felt crestfallen," Fred said decades later, still sound-
ing wounded. "I did my best to bring what I was asked to bring
to people for refreshment, and I'll never forget how that felt. Of
course, I went off and got the correct thing."

In December 1951, only two months after Fred started, NBC
broadcast Gian Carlo Menotti's *Amahl and the Night Visitors*, the
first opera ever written for television. Performed in studio 8H
at Rockefeller Center (later home to *Saturday Night Live*), the
operatic nativity story was so acclaimed that NBC rebroad-
cast it every year through 1965. For Fred Rogers, it was proof
that television programming could aspire to be of the highest
quality.

Meanwhile, Joanne, accompanied by a male friend, paid
a social call on Jim and Nancy Rogers, who were in Florida
on their annual extended winter holiday. She suspected that
Fred's parents told him that she had a new beau, because in
April 1952, she received a letter from Fred proposing marriage.
Joanne quickly decided that her answer was yes, and armed
with a handful of loose change, found a phone booth and called
Fred in New York to accept. Anxiously waiting for Fred to pick

up the phone, she looked at the obscenities scrawled in the phone booth; when he finally answered, she greeted him and then unromantically read a prominent graffito: "Shit." Fred laughed, and when he again asked her to marry him, Joanne quickly agreed. Weeks later, Joanne finished her graduate degree at Florida State and moved up to New York; on July 9, 1952, Fred and Joanne got married.

As a newlywed, Joanne spent her days practicing on the Steinway grand piano and exploring the Upper East Side. At NBC, Fred soon received a promotion to floor manager, meaning that he was responsible for making sure that everything kept moving on a variety of programs (some of them actual variety programs).

"First of all, I timed programs," Fred said. "I had to time a program called *The Voice of Firestone*"—a long-running classical music broadcast—"and that was scary, because we had to get off the air at just the right second."

He floor-managed *The Kate Smith Hour* and *Your Hit Parade*, a chart countdown show (the forerunner of *Solid Gold* or *Top of the Pops*) sponsored by Lucky Strike cigarettes. It had an ensemble of performers singing the hits of the week, including (for a time) Frank Sinatra. After Sinatra left the show in 1950, his replacement was Snooky Lanson. Fred remembered, "Snooky Lanson used to go with the stagehands and play craps behind the set. I'd have to say [stage whisper] 'Mr. Lanson, you're on next!' And he'd say, "Okay, Fred,' get out in front of the thing and do his song. And that'd be over and he'd go back and play again."

Fred also worked closely with Gabby Hayes, a vaudevillian who had remade himself as a star of westerns, often playing the cantankerous sidekick (he was in fifteen John Wayne movies, for example). By the time Fred knew him, he was hosting *The Gabby Hayes Show*, a children's program where he would introduce an old western movie, maybe whittling a piece of wood while he talked. Fred was fascinated by how as soon as the show ended, Hayes would change out of his cowboy duds and into street clothes—or, on the many nights he had opera tickets, into a tuxedo. Fred noted, "Often you don't know the depths of someone you see only on television."

Fred was learning the mechanics of how television programs were made, but Hayes taught him one of the most important lessons of his tenure. Killing time one day while the movie played, Fred asked the show's star, "Mr. Hayes, what do you think of when you look at that camera and know there are thousands of people watching you?"

Hayes extended an index finger and, with a twang, confided, "Freddy, I think of one little buckaroo."

At the time, Fred had no thoughts of ever hosting his own program, but when he did, he remembered and embraced Hayes' philosophy: "When I look at the camera, I think of one person—not any specific person." But the conversation also helped Fred form his philosophy on how television worked. "It's very, very personal, this medium," Fred said. "That's one of the reasons that I thought for education it would be so fabulous. Because if you have someone on television it looks like that person is looking at each person individually. A live teacher can't do that." (Fred was well aware that teachers standing in front of a classroom had other virtues, but he was fascinated by how television was an intimate mass medium.)

Fred's most unusual floor-manager assignment came in

studio 3K, which had the only color TV cameras in New York City. Color broadcasts had an exceptionally limited audience for NBC: they were sent to exactly three TV sets, located in the offices of the chairman of the network, the president of the network, and the CEO of the parent company, RCA. These heavyweights would judge the technology and decide whether the world was ready for color.

For a couple of weeks, Fred was in charge of moving various brightly colored objects around the set—which should have been simple enough, but there was a problem. When somebody told Fred to move the green parrot, he had to ask, "Which one is the green one?" Fred was color-blind, which only added to the absurdity of a television program made for three people—but he was determined to succeed nevertheless. "To have the first floor manager for color television be color-blind, I think, is kind of a whimsical thing," he opined.

Off the job, Fred and Joanne were learning how to live together. Both were accustomed to having their own space, but since they doted on each other, the transition was a happy one. Sometimes Joanne would swing by 30 Rockefeller Plaza to watch Fred wrangling a rehearsal or a live broadcast, and she would always be thrilled by the energy in the room.

One day, Fred remembered, the young couple were walking down Fifth Avenue when they spotted a man on a bicycle: their old Rollins classmate Anthony Perkins, who had moved to New York City to be an actor. Perkins, delighted to see them, got off his bike and spontaneously said, "Come on, let's go to the top of this building."

"I don't remember what building it was, but we went to the roof, he made paper airplanes, and we threw them off the building," Fred said. "I wish that we'd been able to stay close after that. But his was a very different life from the one that I had chosen."

After two years at NBC, Fred was thinking about what he had achieved and what he might be able to accomplish in the future. "I thought television was doing good things," he said. "I was impressed with the musical programs we did. There were still some that . . . I guess there'll always be pie-throwing programs."

In late 1953, Fred's father gave him some important news: a new television station was starting in Pittsburgh. The year before, the Federal Communications Commission had divided the airwaves for local TV stations and had reserved 242 channels across the country for public television (or, as it was often called then, educational television). The Pittsburgh station, WQED, broadcasting on channel 13, would be just the fifth public TV station in the United States, and the first to be community-sponsored. (The previous four had all been affiliated with universities.)

When Fred told some of his NBC friends that he was considering working at WQED, they thought it was folly. As he remembered their advice: "You are nuts! That place isn't even on the air yet. And you're in line to be a producer or a director or anything you want to be here."

He told them, "No, I have a feeling that educational television might be, at least for me, the wave of the future." Fred had enjoyed his time at NBC, but he felt that it was time to move on: "I didn't feel that I could use all the talents that had been given to me as a floor manager," he said, which might be the most polite way ever of expressing frustration with a job.

Fred investigated the educational-television landscape, even flying halfway across the country to visit the University of Iowa, a pioneer in public broadcasting. He applied for a job at WQED: a strong candidate because of his NBC experience, he was hired as program manager, one of the first six employees. In November 1953, Fred, Joanne, and the Steinway grand piano all moved to Pittsburgh.

FRED'S PARENTS WERE DELIGHTED TO HAVE HIM BACK CLOSE TO Latrobe, but Fred hadn't returned to western Pennsylvania because he was homesick: he had calculated that although he was on track to have a successful career at NBC, he had a better chance of getting his ideas on the air at an understaffed, chaotic startup with a desperate need to fill the hours of the broadcast day. Given the chance, he was confident he could make television he would be proud of.

Running the skeleton staff at WQED was Dorothy Daniel, the assistant to Leland Hazard, who was the vice president of Pittsburgh Plate Glass (a successful industrial manufacturer) and the president of the station. Her official job at WQED was promotions director: "I was the only one crazy enough to try it," Daniel said.

When she wasn't fund-raising for the $250,000 the station would need its first year, she was the fledgling station's general manager and resident dynamo. She presided over weekly staff meetings where everyone was encouraged to contribute ideas, including the janitor. The WQED staff worked in a turn-of-the-century mansion across the street from the University of Pittsburgh—the school rented it to WQED on a sweetheart deal of one dollar per year.

Starting at the station just a few weeks before Fred was Josephine Vicari, a Pittsburgh native two years younger than him. Having spent her youth working in her family's Italian restaurants, she was energetic and outgoing. She had come to WQED hoping to perform in a children's show, but while she waited for the station to go on the air, she did secretarial work, helped with fund-raising, and polished an idea she had for a quiz show called *The Greeks Have a Word for It*.

One day, Fred gave her a brochure he had received about some games, thinking it might help her with the quiz show. They started chatting about the children's program that didn't yet exist, except as a blank space on WQED's schedule. Discovering their compatibility, they asked Daniel if they could do the show together, with Fred Rogers as producer and Josephine Vicari as the star.

Daniel immediately agreed to the show, which they called *The Children's Corner*. Vicari said, "Between us, we had about eighty-seven programs we were trying to get Mrs. Daniel to consider, but the only one she wanted us to do was *The Children's Corner*." At Daniel's request, Vicari changed her stage name to one less obviously Italian: Josie Carey.

Their most ambitious idea for the show was to have scenes in an attic, filled with excess furniture and household items, which would come to life and talk. When they could steal time from their other responsibilities, they developed a cast of characters: Lydia Lamp was engaged to Lawrence Light. Gramophone was the attic gossip; a stuffed horse called I Know would only ever say "Iiiii know!" Carey said, "We had a plastic fish whose name was Foo Foo Chanel who talked with a French accent and who was in love with Bill Bookworm." They named the attic segment "It's a Small World"—a full decade before Walt Disney debuted the attraction of the same name at the 1964 World's Fair.

A couple of weeks before WQED went on the air, the station's board of nine men hired William Wood, a former CBS newscaster with a resonant voice. They named him station manager and installed him as Daniel's boss—she had been doing an exemplary job, but the board apparently wanted a man running the joint. One of Wood's first decrees was that he wanted open auditions for *The Children's Corner,* meaning that Fred and Josie had to apply to work on the show they had been busy creating for months.

They wrote a song for the audition (Josie did the lyrics; Fred, the music) called "Why Hi, Don't I Know You." Not only did they keep their jobs, "Why Hi, Don't I Know You" became the theme song of *The Children's Corner.* That should have been the end of any issues—except that soon after, Wood declared a budget crunch and fired a large chunk of the WQED staff, most notably Fred Rogers.

While it appeared that Wood had a vendetta against Fred, his motives may have been purely financial. Other staffers thought that, knowing of the Rogers family wealth, Wood was hoping that Fred would stick around and do the same job as an unpaid volunteer. The firing happened on a Friday, and provoked an immediate mutiny from Josie Carey and Dorothy Daniel, who threatened to quit. Over the weekend, Wood discovered that the Rogers family was close with WQED president Leland Hazard, who sternly warned him not to let Fred go. On Monday, Fred had his job back.

The *Children's Corner* set was constructed as cheaply as possible. Josie would perform in front of a cloth backdrop: basically, a gray canvas tarpaulin painted with childish images of a globe, a mailbox, and a grandfather clock. All the furniture for the attic segment was purchased from Goodwill. According to Josie, their off-camera budget for the show amounted to exactly one yellow legal pad for an entire season of television. "We used it very carefully," she said. "We would do one rundown a day on this sheet of paper, because that's all we had."

On April 1, 1954, WQED went live on channel 13 with an hour-long special. "People had been watching the test pattern for weeks before that," Fred claimed. A full schedule began a few days later, on Monday, April 5. The night of April 4, Dorothy Daniel threw a dinner party at the Pittsburgh Playhouse for all the young WQED staffers who had been toiling ceaselessly to make a new television station. At each plate, there was a small gift chosen by Daniel: Fred's was a striped tiger puppet.

Fred and Josie had planned for a stuffed bird to emerge from their set's painted clock now and then, offering historical facts, but on the day of the show's premiere, they realized that although they had arranged for a slit to be cut in the canvas, they had neglected to get the bird. So Fred stuck the tiger puppet through the slit and announced in a squeaky voice, "It's 5:02 and Columbus discovered America in 1492." They named the puppet Daniel Striped Tiger, in honor of Dorothy Daniel. ("Striped" was pronounced with two syllables.)

Fred and Josie quickly discovered that five hour-long shows made for a *lot* of airtime to fill every week. They had plenty of regular guests, including visits from a "craft lady," who demonstrated easy art projects, and members of the Pittsburgh Symphony, who showed off their instruments. Carey said, "We had a magician come in and teach the children magic. We had a man teach Morse code. We had a tap dancer. We had aerobics, before aerobics was big! We showed them how to make pizza before anyone had heard of pizza!"

Local members of the Junior League would come on for a segment called "Doll's House," where one woman would read a story while the others acted it out with dolls, not with any particular skill. Another regular segment was "The Noisy Party": while somebody played piano for twenty minutes, children would loudly sing songs and bang on pots and pans. A zookeeper from the Pittsburgh Zoo came on once a week to present various animals; for some reason, he kept showing up with snakes.

They had planned to give children introductory lessons in a foreign language—specifically, in French, since Fred was fluent enough in French to pass as a native speaker. WQED management decreed that the language needed to be Spanish, but then got them a series of educational films produced by Ohio State University called *Ein, Zwei, Drei*. So *The Children's Corner* taught the children of Pittsburgh to speak German.

"I combed through the country for free films," Fred said. "We had such things as how you grow grass in New Hampshire. Can you imagine the amount of material you need for an hour a day?"

Many of the films were old and in poor condition, as was WQED's equipment, so movie time often featured technical glitches. While somebody fixed the projector, Josie would need to ad-lib. To help her out, Fred would stick the Daniel Striped Tiger puppet out of the clock. Josie said, "Fred would see that we were in panic time and he'd put the little tiger out and I'd talk to Fred about anything, anything at all."

Daniel might greet Josie by saying, "You must have been thinking seventeen and a half nice thoughts." The human and the tiger would banter about anything that came to mind— what it's like to eat ice cream with a fork, or how lettuce doesn't taste the same when you eat it with a spoon.

"Josie would talk with Daniel as if that was the only person in the room," Fred said. "It was just magical, the way they would converse." He particularly remembered one day when Josie wasn't her usual cheery, effervescent self. "I am so upset," she told Daniel Striped Tiger.

"Well, you just tell me about it," Daniel replied.

"And she just bared her soul to him. This was so real," Fred said decades later, still awed. "I wonder if she knew that we were on the air. The camera was on. She probably did. But she trusted Daniel's ears so, and she trusted her audience so, that she could be her whole self."

Sometimes Josie would become so absorbed in her conversations with Daniel that after the show she would start recounting them to Fred, telling him the wonderful things Daniel had said, quite forgetting that Fred had actually been the one to say them. "In one ear and out her mouth," Fred would say affectionately.

Fred and Josie became fast friends. She liked to tell him

that he was her best friend, which would always prompt him to say in a virtuous tone, "A boy can't have a girl for a best friend!"

"And I'd give him a funny look," Josie said merrily. "We were really very, very close friends." But although they spent most of their days in close collaboration, the purest expression of their friendship came when the camera was on and Fred had a puppet on his hand.

Josie said, "The part of Fred that was gentle and kind and sweet and nice was Daniel. Daniel was incapable of doing anything that wasn't just as good as he could do it. I remember the nicest thing Daniel ever said . . . he was all excited this one day and he said, 'Josie, I saw a flower today and I didn't pick it.' It was early spring and Fred and I had been walking back from lunch and we saw the same flower and we both stopped to admire it and went on to do the program. And that was Daniel saying that it was very tempting. 'I would like to have had that flower. It was a beautiful thing. I saw a flower today and I didn't pick it.'"

Realizing that the show's most magical moments came when Josie was talking to Fred via a puppet, not when children were banging on pots and pans, they decided to include more puppetry. Puppet shows had sustained Fred creatively for countless hours of his lonely childhood, but he hadn't employed those talents for a long time—Joanne didn't even know that he had any affinity for puppets. But now he kept adding new puppets to the *Children's Corner* repertory company.

They pulled some puppets from Fred's old trunk and purchased others. When WQED management relented and said Fred could give French lessons, he decided to do it through puppetry. They bought the show's second puppet: another tiger, Grandpere. "We dressed him up with a little mustache and a beret," Josie said. "He came from France in a box marked 'Third Class Mail' and he arrived as a present from Daniel's pen pal." They gave Grandpere a home by painting the Eiffel Tower on the gray tarp that served as their set.

Fred and Josie developed the personalities and backstories of the puppet characters together, both through planning and on-camera improvisations. Josie named Cornflake S. Pecially, the show's industrious rocking-chair inventor and manufacturer.

Henrietta Pussycat, named after Josie's husband Henry, was a shy black cat who was a pet of the unseen Mister Rogers. She loved to dress up—she starred in her own fashion show twice a year—and her vocabulary leaned heavily on the word "meow." She could say "beautiful," "telephone," and "Mister Rogers"; all other words were rendered as "meow."

Fred bought an owl puppet by mail order and surprised Josie with it one day when they were making a promotional appearance outside the studio. Josie and the owl immediately bonded and were soon singing a song together.  "I've escaped, I've escaped," the owl declared, and so X the Owl (full name: X Scape the Owl) joined the family. X was exuberant, inquisitive, and a fan of Benjamin Franklin—but he needed a place to live.

Fred said, "What we suggested to him was he find an acorn. And so he went, found an acorn, and we Scotch-taped it to the bottom of the set." Over the course of a week, they showed an oak rapidly growing on the set's gray backdrop. "And every day, the art crew would paint a little more of the tree, and finally the tree was completely painted on the set. We had a knothole, opened the knothole, and X came through."

Lady Elaine Fairchilde came from Fred's personal collection: he named her after his sister and turned her into the show's loudmouth truth-teller and troublemaker. "Wouldn't it be funny if Lady Elaine doesn't know she's so ugly?" Josie asked Fred. (The puppet was rather frightful with its ruddy complexion and intense stare.) They played with that idea for a while: "Lady Elaine started out being a professional bridesmaid and she'd say 'Isn't it strange? When I'm at a wedding nobody looks at the bride.' And she'd give her beauty tips—how to grow a wart on the end of your nose and things like that."

King Friday XIII was another puppet from Fred's trunk, purchased on a trip to Europe. Josie gave him his name; Fred came up with his haughty voice. When Fred spoke as King Friday, he pulled his lips back over his teeth and looked like he was gumming a mouthful of particularly stubborn taffy. They decided that the king's birthday would be Friday the thirteenth, to counteract the superstition that it was an unlucky day; anytime they did a show that fell on Friday the thirteenth, they threw a royal birthday party.

Fred and Josie were figuring out what made *The Children's Corner* work by actually doing it, one hour a day, five days a week. That trial-and-error approach, where enthusiasm outweighed experience, permeated WQED. One of the show's cameramen, Joel Dulberg, was just sixteen years old: before the station even launched, he wanted to work there so badly that every day he would ride his bicycle to the WQED office and camp out on the steps until the receptionist yelled at him, telling him to leave.

Eventually Dulberg's persistence got him into the building as an "office boy," but he really wanted to operate a camera. Dulberg said that Fred immediately began to look out for him. "He took a keen interest in my well-being, making sure that I was not left alone too often and that my schoolwork was being taken care of," Dulberg said. Fred sat down with the teenager and explained different paths through the TV industry. Fred and Josie advocated for Dulberg with the engineering staff, so over a period of months, the engineers taught him how to operate the station's heavy cameras. When *The Children's Corner* launched, Dulberg was one of the show's two cameramen. He stayed behind the camera for a year, hustling over to the studio every day after school—and then his family relocated to New York City. Fred put in a good word with his friends at NBC, which hired Dulberg in the news department.

Having changed Joel Dulberg's life forever, Fred stayed in touch with him. Dulberg, who went on to work for the news show *60 Minutes* for over three decades (as a sound mixer), said that Fred Rogers "often told me how proud he was of all my achievements through the years."

"You learn by doing," Fred said. "And we all did a lot." During *Children's Corner* broadcasts, Fred would rush around behind the scenes. He might be speaking with Josie (via a puppet) one moment, and then the next be accompanying her on organ while she sang a song they wrote together, such as "Mimum Polyglottos Is My Pet" or "I Found the Children's Corner." The organ was on the other side of the studio, so he would run over, clutching the loose change in his pocket to make sure that the microphones wouldn't pick up a jingling sound. Fred discovered that his hard-soled shoes were audible when he ran across the old wooden floor of the studio, so he developed a daily ritual: before every show, he would sit down, take off his shoes, and put on a pair of sneakers.

Lacking Nielsen ratings, they used viewer mail as a barometer of their popularity. After the first week of shows, William Wood, the WQED station manager, grudgingly informed Fred and Josie that they had received sixty-eight letters that day, while none of the station's other shows had received any—which he found all the more puzzling, since he didn't think the two of them were particularly talented.

They incorporated the mail into the show. Every day, "Josie sang the opening song, and then she showed pictures that kids had sent in," Fred said. When Daniel Striped Tiger encouraged viewers to join a *Children's Corner* fan club, called the Tame Tiger Torganization, they got as many as 750 letters a day. The TTT offered members four stripes for mastering various tasks; the last one was awarded for memorizing the club's song, with French lyrics by Fred, "Je Suis un Tigre Apprivoisé," which translated to English as "I Am a Tame Tiger."

They invited four-stripe members of the TTT to a birthday party for Daniel, which they arbitrarily declared to be July 12. Expecting only a handful of children, they were stunned by the hundreds who showed up, forming a line that extended down the block. They took the refreshments and divided each serving among eight guests. The highlight was when the throng of children sang "Je Suis un Tigre Apprivoisé," enthusiastically and perfectly.

The Children's Corner had regular visitors, like the snake-loving zookeeper and an English woman, Emily Jacobson, who volunteered to read poetry on the air. "When you're doing an hour a day, you're mighty glad for people to arrive on your doorstep," Fred said. But it also had surprise guests, sometimes celebrities and future stars who were in Pittsburgh for other reasons, such as pianist Van Cliburn, actress Shirley Jones (not yet famous for movie musicals or *The Partridge Family*, she was Josie Carey's former roommate), and comedian Johnny Carson, who had not yet taken over *The Tonight Show*—he spoke gently, if not especially amusingly, with the puppets.

Also appearing was Charles Schulz, creator of the *Peanuts* newspaper strip. Like Fred, he was a sympathetic chronicler of the fears and traumas of childhood, and the creator of a fractious ensemble of characters, each one expressing an aspect of his own personality, from awkward to imperious. But he was too uncomfortable on camera to realize the affinity. Josie said he was just as timid as his creation, Charlie Brown. "He just seemed like he was afraid to be part of it," she said sadly. "He didn't know what he should say; he wasn't sure he should be there."

The most memorable guest may have been Gertrude Berg, the pioneering creator and star of the long-running show about an upwardly mobile Jewish family called *The Goldbergs*, a hit on both radio and television. When she appeared on *The Children's Corner*, she marched in front of the camera wearing a long sable coat and jumped into conversation with Henrietta Pussycat; the two of them traded their favorite recipes for blintzes. Then Berg pointed at a castle painted on the backdrop and demanded, "Who lives there?" Informed that it was occupied by King Friday XIII, Berg declared, "I want to meet him."

"The king came out, there was fanfare," Fred recalled. The king examined his visitor and asked, "Have you ever been presented at court before, Mrs. Berg?"

Berg replied, "Only night court, Your Majesty."

Another person who eventually appeared in front of the *Children's Corner* cameras, with some misgivings: Fred Rogers. It was one thing to be crouched behind the backdrop, conversing with Josie in the guise of a shy tiger. It was quite another to appear on camera in a tuxedo and a black velvet crown, descending from the ceiling while suspended by wires, but he did, billed as "Prince Charming."

Josie said, "He had a modern castle in the sky. He came down from the clouds and he taught ballroom dancing—he danced with me. And then he taught jitterbug! It's hard to believe, but he did."

To play Prince Charming, Fred insisted that he needed to wear a domino mask—nevertheless, his appearances were so popular that Prince Charming briefly had a spinoff show called *The Prince,* airing at noon on WQED. Other characters on that show included Ticker the Elf and Parmazelle Turtel.

Also appearing on the airwaves of WQED in 1954: Dr. Benjamin Spock, who taught the subject of child development across the street at the University of Pittsburgh and cofounded the nearby Arsenal Family & Children's Center. Since Spock was also the author of the mega-bestseller *Baby and Child Care,* NBC sent a scout to Pittsburgh to see if his weekly program, *Parents and Dr. Spock,* was worth picking up for a national audience. The scout wasn't impressed by the doctor, but while visiting the WQED building, she caught an episode of *The Children's Corner* and was so taken by it, she brought a kinescope copy of the show back to New York City and recommended that NBC acquire the series.

NBC soon offered Fred and Josie a summer job: Would they like to do a Saturday-morning edition of *The Children's Corner* for four weeks, filling in for ventriloquist Paul Winchell while he went on vacation? Josie's answer was yes, without reservations—this was the step into the big time that she had dreamed of. Fred wasn't so sure: he knew all too well the compromises that commercial television could involve. But he agreed to return to NBC for four weeks, starting in August 1955.

The Children's Corner aired in the same block of programming as *The Pinky Lee Show*. Burlesque star Pinky Lee embodied exactly the type of television that Fred didn't want to make: slapstick, pie-throwing, machine-gun banter. Pinky Lee's signature line: "Oooooh! You make me so mad!" But the gentle approach of a shy tiger proved more successful than a blast of seltzer in the face. "We broke a record for how much mail they got," Josie said. "I think they got 138,000 letters." After the four-week run, NBC wanted *The Children's Corner* to return to its Saturday-morning schedule as a regular series.

Fred and Josie asked Leland Hazard, the president of WQED, to negotiate their contract—which would have been a blatant conflict of interest, except that Fred and Josie (mostly Fred) had declared that they didn't want to leave WQED. The duo didn't haggle over the production money; they didn't ask for higher salaries, long-term guaranteed contracts, or guest spots on *The Tonight Show*. Josie said that the only point they insisted on was "you can't make us move from Pittsburgh. The NBC lawyers just looked at each other like we were out of our minds."

Every week, starting on December 24, 1955, Fred and Josie

did an hour-long *Children's Corner* on WQED Monday through Thursday. They left for New York on Friday morning, performed a half-hour *Children's Corner* on Saturday morning that was broadcast nationwide by NBC, and then flew back to Pittsburgh on Saturday afternoon. The result, Josie said ruefully, was that they didn't make the most of their golden opportunity: "They wanted to introduce us to the journalists and the people who would do promotions and publicity, but Fred wanted to get back to Pittsburgh to go to church on Sunday morning!" She was Christian herself, having been raised Catholic, but wasn't as devout as Fred—she found his intensity of faith both irksome and admirable.

"I was always so envious of him because he looked forward to going to church. I didn't know another grown man who couldn't wait for Sunday to go to church!" Josie said. "But Fred, you know: *church, church, church.*" She finally visited his church to see what all the Presbyterian fuss was about and conceded that they did have a wonderful minister.

NBC manufactured new versions of Fred's puppet collection: larger ones, so they would be easier to see on television. Otherwise, the executives mostly left *The Children's Corner* to its own devices. Fred and Josie didn't book guests on NBC, and they couldn't read books on the air (copyright issues), so they mostly had human-puppet conversations. They had to run their songs by the network ahead of time, which sometimes resulted in arguments. The NBC lawyer thought that Fred and Josie's song "You're Special" was too similar to Cole Porter's "You're the Top." But when NBC said that they couldn't perform one of their signature songs, "Goodnight, God," because of its religious content, Fred balked.

"Well, then, I don't think we'll come back," he told them. NBC checked the ratings and quickly backed down.

While Fred and Josie would loosely outline what might happen on the show before they went on the air, they also liked to surprise each other. One Saturday morning on NBC, King Friday labored mightily before producing an enormous dictionary. "He was giving me a royal test," Josie recalled, "and he said that if I passed this test that meant I had royal blood or something. So he said, 'This is the test,' and he handed me this enormous dictionary. And he said, 'Tell me the word that I'm thinking of. Find the word that I'm thinking of in this dictionary.'" Confronted with the preposterous image of the king brandishing a dictionary many times larger than his own puppet body and the impossibility of guessing the word, Josie started laughing hysterically. The studio crew also broke into laughter—and got chewed out for it by NBC management, since they were supposed to document the program stoically.

In the spring of 1956, Fred and Josie were called into the office of an NBC vice president. He complimented them on the quality of *The Children's Corner* and said, "My child is so invested in that program, I figure that it can't be for the masses."

"It was so bizarre," Fred said of the VP's logic. Even in the earliest days of television, the executives who put shows on the air had contempt for the people who watched them—an attitude that Fred couldn't fathom. He had too much respect for the children in his audience to condescend to them. Nevertheless, the message was clear: they would finish their contract and not come back. Their last NBC broadcast was April 20, 1956.

Josie Carey made one more trip to New York City on behalf of *The Children's Corner:* it won a prestigious Sylvania Award (a

1950s TV honor that then rivaled the Emmys) for the best lo-cally produced television show. "It was just the most exciting night of my life," she said. Broadway star Mary Martin and famous newspaper columnist Earl Wilson sat near her, and comedian Phil Silvers shook her hand. But she had to bring a friend with her on the train trip to New York. "Fred would not go with me to collect that award," she said. "He did not want to go to that party."

Fred Rogers, twenty-eight years old when *The Children's Corner* ended its NBC run, had been thinking about what was most important to him—and it wasn't making small talk with celeb-rities in evening wear. The more time he spent in Pittsburgh, the more he felt that his decision to leave New York City had been the correct one. "It gave me a chance to use all the talents that I had ever been given," he said of his work at WQED. "I loved children, I loved drama, I loved music, I loved whimsy, I loved puppetry." As fulfilled as he was doing *The Children's Corner* five days a week, he felt ready to commit more deeply to his beliefs—so he finally enrolled in the seminary.

He had been admitted to the Western Theological Seminary in Pittsburgh years earlier; when he contacted the seminary, he found that not only were the school's doors still open to him, the administration was amenable to his enrolling part-time so he could keep working at WQED.

On his first day at school, trying to figure out how much education he could squeeze into his lunch hour, he asked the admissions office staff, "If you were starting your theological education right here and now, and you had time to take only one course, what would that course be?"

They didn't hesitate. "Oh, Bill Orr's Systematic Theology."

Dr. William Orr proved to be one of the greatest influences on Fred Rogers' worldview, both through his formal teachings and his personal example. "Three or four days a week," Fred said, "I would leave the frantic life of television production and drive to the seminary to study with a person who not only taught Christian theology—he lived it. Oh, we learned about epistemology and Christology, and eschatology, sanctification, and justification, and existentialism, but most of all, we witnessed the unfolding of the life of one of God's saints."

Fred paid close attention to how sometimes Orr would go to lunch in the freezing Pittsburgh winter and return without his coat—not because he had lost it, but because he had given it away to a homeless person. Orr would shrug off the selfless donation, saying that he had other coats at home.

One time, Fred asked Orr about a hymn he had sung in church the previous Sunday, "A Mighty Fortress Is Our God," which declares that the singer will stand stoutly against "the prince of darkness grim," because "one little word shall fell him." Fred's question: "Dr. Orr, what is that one little word that would wipe out evil?"

"Fred, it's 'forgiveness,'" his mentor said without hesitation. "The only thing that evil cannot stand is forgiveness. It simply disintegrates in the presence of forgiveness."

Orr emphasized a personal philosophy that was governed by kindness, generosity, and, yes, forgiveness, rather than adherence to a detailed moral code. With those ideals, Orr believed, the good Christian could enjoy the serendipity of life, with all its changes and surprises, rather than walling oneself off from new experiences, new friendships, new possibilities. Fred made these values his own, not because he wanted to present himself as a paragon of virtue, but because they made his life better and fuller.

Fred took classes at the seminary with professors other than Dr. Orr, of course. "With only one course a semester," he said, "little by little I was able to study systematic theology, Greek and Hebrew, church history, homiletics, everything." He would come to work at WQED early, then take a break sometime in the morning to drive over to the seminary.

One of those courses, a class in general counseling, was with the school's dean, Gordon Jackson. To be better able to help their future parishioners, students were required to work with one person for a whole semester, meeting with them and discussing their problems at least once a week. Fred immediately asked if he could work with a child instead of an adult.

The answer was yes—if his work was supervised by Dr. Margaret McFarland. She was the director of the prestigious Arsenal Family & Children's Center, which she had cofounded with Dr. Benjamin Spock; it provided early education for the children of Pittsburgh and served as a site for Pitt students to study child development.

McFarland was a small woman with a gentle air and utter conviction in her own beliefs—steel rebar wrapped in a string of pearls. Her technique as a professor at the University of Pittsburgh: She would invite a mother and child to class, and start by letting her students watch them interact for fifteen minutes. The rest of the class—over two hours—would be filled with McFarland's observations from that interlude.

The notion that children were emerging people with their own psychological needs, not wild beasts that needed to be disciplined or empty vessels to fill with information, was still

shockingly new. Spock was its most famous proponent, starting with the 1946 publication of *The Common Sense Book of Baby
and Child Care*—and so, in some quarters, he was demonized
for encouraging a loosey-goosey, overpermissive parenting
style. (Rogers, later in life, would face similar criticism from
people who thought paying attention to children and telling
them they were special was by definition overindulgent.)

McFarland was never as famous as Spock—she published
very little, focusing on teaching—but according to their Arsenal colleagues, she was every bit as brilliant. She weaved
together a lifetime of hands-on experience with teaching, a
solid grounding in psychoanalysis, and a deep knowledge of
the academic literature, extemporizing monologues in which
she would travel from an anecdote about monsters under the
bed to overarching theories of child development.

McFarland believed that "attitudes aren't taught, they're
caught." Fred had a story he liked to tell about her teaching
technique: "She once invited a well-known sculptor from the
faculty of Carnegie Institute of Technology (now Carnegie
Mellon University) to come to our nursery school. Dr. Mc-
Farland said to him, 'I don't want you to teach sculpting. All I
want you to do is to love clay in front of the children.' And that's
what he did. He came once a week for a whole term, sat with
the four- and five-year-olds as they played, and he 'loved' his
clay in front of them. The adults who have worked at that center for many years have said that not before or since have the
children in that school used clay so imaginatively as when they
had those visits from the sculptor who obviously delighted in
his medium."

From Fred's perspective, the moral of the story was that

teaching, like most good things in the world, is built on honesty and enthusiasm. But we can see something else: just as the sculptor galvanized the children, Margaret McFarland's passion for a rigorous but empathetic approach to child development inspired Fred Rogers not just to follow her studies, but to incorporate them into his life's work.

As an apprentice at the Arsenal, Fred was told to call his sessions with children "play interviews" because, as Dr. McFarland told her students, "You are not trained therapists; you are trained observers and listeners." They were not only helping the children with their presence, they were learning how, say, a girl playing with blocks might be showing them what was happening in her own life.

Fred said, "There was one little boy who did everything he could to turn every man he met into an abusive father. Because of his home situation, that's all that he knew from men, so that's what he had learned to expect. That boy was a master of being able to get me just to the edge of being very angry. Then I would remember, thanks to my supervision, that this is exactly what he was trying to do, and I must never give in, because one of the best things I could do for that boy was to let him know that all men are not abusive."

Fred and the boy spent a lot of time together playing with puppets, helping the child work through his issues and reducing his hostility. "We helped each other grow," Fred said.

At home, Fred and Joanne were blissful in each other's company. Their first child, James Rogers (sometimes Jamie, sometimes Jim), was born on September 4, 1959. Joanne said, "We were a not-so-young mother and father, both thirty-one years old, when our first son was born. We'd been married for seven years, and were overjoyed to be a family at last. I can also remember how insecure Fred and I both felt over the prospect of taking care of this tiny person." They did just fine; twenty-one months later, on June 18, 1961, they had a second son, John Rogers.

Meanwhile, Josie Carey was also branching out from WQED. Pittsburgh had one other television station, the commercial broadcaster KDKA, then a CBS affiliate. KDKA invited her to host *another* children's show for them in the mornings, which she did: *Josie's Story Land*. She allowed that she was probably the most recognizable person in Pittsburgh at that point: "Only two stations in the city, and I was on both of them!"

At KDKA, she had a wisecracking cohost, Sterling Yates; a cartoon in the middle of the show; and a talented jazz pianist named Johnny Costa, who sometimes dressed up in a lion costume or in a dress. Occasionally she would get delayed at KDKA and Fred would have to start *The Children's Corner* without her. Whenever that happened, he would call up Ernie Coombs in the WQED art department and ask him to ad-lib on camera until Josie arrived.

WQED didn't object to Josie appearing on another station, so long as she kept starring in *The Children's Corner* and producing her quiz show *The Greeks Have a Word for It* for them—but they cut her salary of sixty-five dollars per week, since she now had a second source of income. "They thought I could live on their fifty dollars instead of sixty-five, so they took my fifteen and gave it to Fred," she remembered indignantly. "They said, 'Well, that's because he's a family man.' Well, Fred didn't need it!" she objected, alluding to his family's wealth.

Fred and Joanne had been spending their summers in Nantucket—the island off the coast of Massachusetts—with his old boss at NBC, Kirk Browning, and Kirk's wife, Barbara. Their 1959 vacation was in the remote town of Madaket, in an old farmhouse with eight hundred feet of beachfront. At the end of the summer, Kirk discovered the house was for sale. He loved it, but since he couldn't afford it, he told Fred about its availability.

"Fred went to his family, who helped him buy the house," Kirk said. "I can't tell you what the house is worth today. Then over the years, he bought all the land around the house." The house was structurally sound, but leaned a bit. Fred and Joanne called it "The Crooked House," and it became the site of an annual retreat with their children, a place of rest and renewal.

Josie admired Fred and regarded his eccentricities with affection. "Fred sometimes didn't want to have any connection with the outside world," she said. "He took the radio out of his car. Most people have a radio put in; Fred had his taken out." He watched television just once a week, and then only for a few minutes: he would tune into the beginning of *Alfred Hitchcock Presents*, because he loved the portentous way the famed director delivered his trademark opening line, "Good evening."

Now the producer and the star were arguing more often. "His mother always said she could tell when we'd had an argument, because we were so insufferably nice to each other on the air," Josie said. "We fought one day—" and then she corrected herself. "Not fought. You never fought with Fred. He says 'oh no' and that's the end of it." But they had a heated twenty-minute debate over whether she should deliver one of her lines using the verb "would," "could," or "should." She could see that her friend was changing, not just in being a stickler for grammar, but in fundamental ways.

"He was starting to feel a call," Josie said. "He started to get quieter and he started to get more interested in the child's reaction." His approach to their show now reflected the influence of Margaret McFarland: "She was educating him about children's needs and what they needed him to focus on. Whereas I was always trying to entertain."

Josie learned how much their viewpoints had diverged on the day when she told him about a gag she had done on *Josie's Story Land* with her cohost, Sterling Yates—part of a running joke where he would hand off a finger puppet of a baby monkey (called Fenwick Bitty-Bit-Bit) to a guest, but then deliberately drop it and say accusingly, "You dropped my baby!"

Yates "was the total opposite of Fred," Josie said. "He'd do anything for a laugh."

Recently, Yates had announced on camera that he had lost his "baby."

"What was the last place you saw it?" Josie asked

He replied deadpan, "I think it's in the glove compartment of a car that was headed to Cleveland."

Since *Josie's Story Land* was syndicated in Cleveland, the children there sent them random objects in the mail, asking, "Is this your baby?" When Josie told Fred about this bit, which she thought of as goofy fun, he was appalled.

"Do you realize that is one of the worst things you can tell a child?" he asked her. "Why, a child is so afraid of being left or lost. And it's such an enclosed space, the glove compartment. The child is going to feel that he's going to be put in a situation where he's in a small place and he's lost his parents." Josie defended herself, saying that it was just a silly joke, and kids knew it wasn't real. Fred wasn't having it: "He just thought it was horrible."

Josie's first allegiance was to entertainment; Fred's highest priority was the emotional well-being of children. For years, their values had been congruent enough to do an hour of television five days a week, but now they discovered just how different they were.

In late 1961, Fred told Josie that he wanted to end *The Children's Corner*: he was in his final year at the seminary, and he needed to concentrate on his academic work. Left unsaid was that his aspirations for children's television now exceeded what he could do on *The Children's Corner*. Josie's understanding was that he was leaving television altogether, and that after he was ordained, he would have his own congregation. "For one show to continue on daily for seven years is a long time. We finally just ran out of steam," she said sadly. Josie left WQED and started doing an afternoon show at KDKA called *Funsville*.

Fred, meanwhile, graduated from the seminary in the spring of 1962. He said that he had been "expecting to produce a program for the Presbyterian church." As he remembered it, the church elders had a vague desire to get into television, but "the day before commencement, I found out they weren't able to raise the money to do a program for the church."

His friend the Reverend Bill Barker remembered a somewhat more complicated situation: Fred wanted his ministry to be in the form of a TV show, both because he was uncomfortable preaching in a church and because he thought that he could do the most good for children through the medium of television. The elders of the Pittsburgh Presbytery, an old-fashioned bunch of men, didn't want to ordain him unless he was headed for a traditional pulpit.

Barker appealed personally to the members of the presbytery: "Look, here's an individual who has his pulpit proudly in front of a TV camera. His congregation are little people from the ages of about two or three on up to about seven or eight. And this is a whole congregation of hundreds of thousands if not millions of kids, and this is a man who has been authentically called by the Lord as much as any of you guys."

Somewhat nervously, the elders agreed to the unconventional plan: they would let Rogers minister to children through the cathode-ray tube. "I was ordained by the Pittsburgh Presbytery to work with families through the mass media. It's the only ordination I know of that kind," Fred said. "Because the program was already established, they knew that this was a decent pulpit. They knew that I wasn't overly religious in what I was doing, but I think they believed that the Holy Spirit was operative in the work, and that's what matters." Fred wasn't ordained until June 9, 1963—a year after he graduated from the seminary. By then, he had already left the United States.

While working on *The Children's Corner*, Fred Rogers had been corresponding with another Fred: Fred Rainsberry, the man in charge of children's programming at the Canadian Broadcasting Corporation. The CBC was Canada's first TV network, a public broadcaster that had been airing TV shows since 1950, including children's fare such as *Maggie Muggins*, *Bim Bam Boom*, and *Let's Go to the Museum*. Under Rainsberry's leadership, the CBC favored the gentle, whimsical shows that appealed to Fred Rogers—not the cartoons and pie-throwing he found so abhorrent. Rainsberry himself was a professor of philosophy at the University of Toronto. With his care, some of Fred and Josie's projects had a second life north of the border: after they staged a short musical production of Edward Lear's nineteenth-century nonsense poem "The Owl and the Pussy-cat," the CBC did a version of it.

Fred Rogers was hoping that he could convince the CBC to mount the opera he had been working on since his student days at Rollins, *Josephine the Short-Neck Giraffe*. He wrote letters to Rainsberry encouraging him to consider *Josephine* and offering to drive to Toronto during his summer break to work on it at the CBC headquarters. Rainsberry, for his part, politely told the composer that the dramatic stakes needed to be raised: if having a longer neck was not of the utmost importance for Josephine, he explained, the whole opera would be like a mouthful of soggy bread.

Josephine didn't make it onto the Canadian airwaves; instead, Rainsberry commissioned Fred to write a musical special called *The Peaceable Kingdom*. The two men became friends; Fred Rogers sent funny letters to Canada, and Rainsberry sometimes called Fred at his home. "You'll never know what your phone call did for my spirits the other night!" Fred wrote in a 1961 letter. "It had been a big day of plannings and doings and I had come home to wonder if man wasn't really meant to just sit by his own fire and develop a craft which could be easily carried out at home. Whittling was very tempting at the moment. (But I don't know the first thing about whittling.)"

In another letter, Fred updated Rainsberry on his domestic life: "Joanne is very well. She's such a good mother: she should have a dozen children," he wrote. Then he dryly noted, "She thinks differently about same."

A year later, having just received his master of divinity degree but still not knowing anything about whittling, Fred got another unexpected call from Rainsberry. As Fred told the story, "The day after commencement, I had a call from Fred Rainsberry saying 'I want to produce a new fifteen-minute program to go back to back with Bob Homme's *The Friendly Giant*. And I'd like you to do it.'"

Fred jumped at the opportunity. He recruited his friend Ernie Coombs, who had sometimes filled in for Josie on camera when she was late, to come to Canada with him as the show's assistant puppeteer. He wanted to use the puppet characters from *The Children's Corner*, so he asked Josie to sign over her rights as cocreator. She did so without any qualms—"Fred was almost my minister; I was going to trust him"—but later regretted it when she discovered that she had also given up the rights to the songs they had written together. (That didn't have any financial ramifications; the pair had naïvely signed away the income from their songs to the company that put out a *Children's Corner* record album. But she was dismayed to realize that she no longer had any say in how the songs were used.)

Fred had assumed that Rainsberry was hiring him to do the same job for the children of Canada that he had been doing for the children of Pittsburgh: produce a television show where he would also serve as puppeteer and play the organ behind the scenes. But after he moved to Toronto with Joanne and their boys, Rainsberry told him that he wanted him to appear on camera: "I've seen you talk with kids, Fred, and I want to translate that to television." Fred was reluctant, but eventually Rainsberry persuaded him that he would be the best representative of his own point of view. Rainsberry instructed him, "I want you to look into the lens and just pretend that's a child."

So Fred did just that. Rainsberry gave the show, which debuted on the CBC in late 1962, the awkward title of *Misterogers*.

At age thirty-four, Fred became Mister Rogers. To comple-
ment his experience with television production, puppetry,
and music, he had added a new understanding of the principles of child development. He had always had a deep empathy
for children, rooted in his own youthful memories, but his
years of experience at the Arsenal Family & Children's Center
had given him rigor. He now wrote scripts instead of laying
out loose scenarios that would spark improvisation—and the
scripts addressed the childhood fears and issues that he had
witnessed up close.

He also made sure to delineate transitions in the show very
clearly: Mister Rogers began every episode by changing out
of a suit jacket and into a zip-up sweater, ritually marking the
beginning of his show. The sweaters were from his personal
wardrobe, which meant that they were all Christmas presents
knitted by his mother. Wearing them, Mister Rogers presented
himself as a mature adult, not a child or a clown—but a relaxed,
understanding grown-up.

Daniel Striped Tiger still lived in a clock and X the Owl still
lived in a tree, but now the puppets occupied their own district,
dubbed the Neighborhood of Make-Believe. Canadian scenic
artists built three-dimensional homes for the puppets—most
impressively, King Friday XIII's castle. Mister Rogers had a
house of his own, not in the Neighborhood of Make-Believe
(but with a different layout from the one that would become
familiar on later shows).

The show introduced other inventions that would become
staples of Mister Rogers' television world, including Picture-
Picture, a screen that could display text messages, still images, or films, as necessary. (While this is commonplace in

the twenty-first century, it seemed magical in the 1960s.) Chugging its way through the background was a toy trolley on a track, reminiscent of the trolleys that had provided mass transit in Latrobe when Fred Rogers was growing up. Because the show was Canadian, the trolley sported a sign with the spelling NEIGHBOURHOOD—technically, the puppets lived in the Neighbourhood of Make-Believe.

Misterogers was only fifteen black-and-white minutes, but with all these elements—plus the songs and the even-tempered, encouraging presence of Mister Rogers himself—it contained most of the essential ingredients of *Mister Rogers' Neighborhood*. The bulk of the Canadian show took place in the Neighbourhood of Make-Believe: Mister Rogers appeared on camera in his "real" house for segments at the beginning and end that framed the show.

Mister Rogers would start the show by singing a song and changing into his cardigan, after which he might eat a bowl of cereal, speak to a monkey in French, or turn off the studio lights and look for the home viewer with a flashlight. Again and again, he told the children watching that they were special and he liked them exactly the way they were. The trolley was not yet the bridge to the Neighbourhood of Make-Believe: to make the transition from reality to fantasy, Mister Rogers would pull out a telescope and look through it, and the scene would then dissolve to Make-Believe.

In the Neighbourhood of Make-Believe, X the Owl could graduate from correspondence school, Henrietta Pussycat could appear on the cover of *Feline Fashion* magazine, or King Friday could mandate that anyone visiting his castle was required to wear a hat. With Fred manning the puppets, an array of Canadian actors came through the studio to interact with them—most often Allan Blye, who went on to a successful career in Hollywood, writing and producing for the Smothers Brothers and Sonny and Cher. Also appearing occasionally: Josie Carey, whom Fred convinced to visit Canada during her vacation time.

Carey enjoyed her visits with old friends, both flesh and cloth, although she had to get used to working from a script instead of just having a conversation with Daniel Striped Tiger. On one episode, she made popcorn—but overloaded the popper, so kernels came spilling over the side. She thought it was a delightful TV moment, but Fred insisted on reshooting. He said it might be scary for children, but perhaps more to the point, it wasn't what he had planned.

Misterogers was paired with another fifteen-minute show, *The Friendly Giant*. That program, which starred Bob Homme as a giant named Friendly who lived in a castle with a rooster and a giraffe, lasted on the CBC for over twenty-five years. Fred surely took note of the show's memorable opening: a camera establishing the world of the show by panning over a miniature village. (When the camera reached the giant's oversized boot, Friendly would tell viewers to "Look up—way up!")

Mister Rogers, who had avoided appearing on camera, quickly acclimated to it. He remembered Gabby Hayes' philosophy of speaking to just "one little buckaroo." And he was so busy with his multitudinous off-camera responsibilities on the show—writing scripts and songs, directing, producing, puppeteering—that he didn't have time to dwell on his nerves.

The hard work and long hours at the studio paid off—the show was a huge success with Canadian kids. The Rogers family settled happily into Toronto; Fred even began psychoanaly-sis. Francis Chapman, a CBC director who worked on the show, said, "He told me that his analyst had found him so interesting that he took him on for free—which wasn't necessary for Fred, but it was nice."

The only real blemish on his time in Canada was that his younger son, John, went through a series of painful mishaps: a broken jaw, a leg that got burned by boiling coffee, hernia surgery. Fred could help thousands of children he didn't know with their fears and anxieties, but he couldn't always protect his own family from the world's traumas. In general, as a fa-ther, he was as gentle and empathetic as viewers of his show might imagine—so much so, Joanne had to be in charge of dis-ciplining their boys.

Misterogers had been airing on the CBC for about a year and a half when the Rogers family realized their visas would soon expire. Fred and Joanne had to choose: Would they apply for Canadian citizenship and commit to Toronto for the long term, or would they head back to the United States? "It was a tough decision," Fred said. He loved Toronto, and the show he was making, but he and Joanne decided they wanted to raise their children in the States. *Misterogers* ended its CBC run in the spring of 1964, and the Rogers family returned to Pitts-burgh a few months after that. "I had nothing to come back to in broadcasting," he said, "but I did have a job to come back to in the church."

Ernie Coombs, his assistant puppeteer, stayed in Toronto and kept working for the CBC. Like Mister Rogers, he made the transition to appearing on camera, developing a character called Mr. Dressup and starring in a beloved show of the same name for three decades. Mister Rogers, it turned out, could be inspirational for adults as well as children.

BACK IN THE U.S.A., FRED WENT TO WORK FOR THE PRESBYTERIAN Church's United Oakland Ministry—Oakland was the bustling neighborhood in Pittsburgh that contained the University of Pittsburgh campus and the WQED studio—taking charge of its educational programs. He also tried to bring the *Misterogers* program to the American airwaves. After a decade of making children's television, he had finally figured out the program he wanted to do, the show that he believed could best help young viewers.

The problem was money—an ordinary obstacle for most people, but a new challenge for Fred Rogers. Wealth had never mattered much to him, but he had been able to make career decisions without worrying about the salary that would result, and when he had yearned for something material, from a grand piano to a summer cottage, his family had bought it for him. When Fred returned to the United States, he was able to buy a large, beautiful house in the desirable East End of Pittsburgh. But the price tag of a television series was out of reach.

Then Fred got an unexpected phone call, as if a higher force wanted to demonstrate the concept of divine providence. On the line was George Hill, a Pittsburgh advertising man who was looking for a program that the Joseph Horne department store could sponsor. Horne's, the second-biggest department store in Pittsburgh, wanted a show that would appeal to families and encourage visits during the Christmas shopping season. The only problem was that Fred was adamantly opposed to ads. "I disapprove of hosts of children's programming pitching anything," he explained. "Because they're to be trusted by the children and they're not to use that to be hucksters."

Amazingly, Horne's agreed to his terms: they would pay for the show, with just a brief message at the beginning and end of each fifteen-minute program touting their sponsorship. The show was slated for thirteen episodes, to run on Sundays from October through December 1964, on the ABC affiliate WTAE, broadcasting on channel 4. Guitarist Joe Negri, who provided music for the children's programming on WTAE, was named musical director and provided background music.

After a few episodes, Fred invited Negri to appear on camera: "How would you like to walk through the Neighborhood and just talk to some of the puppets?" Negri was amenable. When casting people to appear on his shows, Fred valued temperament and musical ability just as much as acting talent.

Negri said that Fred had to remain vigilant against the expectation that a program on a commercial station would have, you know, commercials. "Fred and commercial television weren't meant to be," he said, noting Fred's unwillingness to hawk cereal and G.I. Joe action figures. "He was always fighting with the sales department!"

Fred said that he succumbed to the sales department's entreaties, but just once, and only with a puppet on his hand. He decided that it wouldn't violate his compact with children if King Friday expressed his approval of a particular cookie by saying, "Yes, it's berry berry good."

"That's the only commercial that I think I've ever done," Fred said. "I'm so concerned, particularly about selling things to children. I would have never done it on my own. I would have said 'I'm going home' if they said it had to be Fred who did it."

And in fact, for the next four decades, he didn't let his puppets be pitchmen, either. He recognized that he was unusually fortunate to be able to stick to his principles (aside from one berry cookie) and still have a career in television.

The ad-free show, *Misterogers' Neighborhood* (a tweak of the CBC title), delivered for the Joseph Horne department store: "Horne's got all kinds of rave reviews as a result" of not larding the show with commercials, Hill said. They weren't interested, however, in an ongoing sponsorship of the series, especially not a daily half-hour version.

So Mister Rogers headed back to WQED. Working the connections of Hill, WQED president Leland Hazard, and his own family, he pulled together just enough money for a hundred half-hour episodes. The CBC gave him permission to reuse the segments from the Neighbourhood of Make-Believe, which provided a huge cost savings: for those first hundred episodes, he needed to film only half a program.

Fred needed to fill some key staff positions, including props master—a job where the main qualification was being persuasive enough to borrow items from local businesses. A friend recommended David Newell, a University of Pittsburgh graduate who had lived in Hawaii before relocating to England. Fred wired him a job offer in England; he accepted and flew back. Joining a skeleton staff, Newell helped out wherever he could, handling public relations for the show.

The show also needed a musical director, and Fred thought very highly of Johnny Costa, the jazz pianist who had filled that role so well on Josie Carey's show *Josie's Story Land*. Carey said that Costa was a blend of the three principal Marx brothers: a cigar smoker like Groucho, a piano player like Chico, a girl chaser like Harpo. Costa had grown up during the Depression; when his father had trouble finding work, young Johnny could play the accordion well enough to feed the family. After graduating from high school in 1940, he played piano with a big band in New York City, earning a reputation as "the white Art Tatum." But after Pearl Harbor, Costa left the band, got married, and enlisted, in short order. He was part of the Normandy invasion (as an infantry medic); after the war, he gave up the life of a touring musician, staying in Pittsburgh so he could be with his family.

Fred took Costa out to lunch and told him about the job, cautioning him that he didn't have much money.

"How much money *do* you have?" Costa asked.

"For the music budget, I have five thousand dollars," Rogers told him.

"That's exactly what my son needs for the next year of college," Costa said. "I'll do it."

Misterogers' Neighborhood (black-and-white, a half hour long) debuted on WQED in 1965. Initially broadcast only in Pittsburgh (every weekday at 4:30 P.M.), it soon got picked up by the Eastern Educational Television Network, a small consortium of public television stations that also handled Julia Child's *The French Chef*.

The show initially had three sets: the living room, the kitchen, and King Friday's throne room. (The Neighborhood of Make-Believe didn't need to be constructed right away, because the program drew on the CBC library of segments.) The traffic light in the living room would flash when King Friday wished to summon an audience. The boundaries between reality and Make-Believe were more permeable in the early

days: Mister Rogers took phone calls from
the Neighborhood of Make-Believe and
sometimes discussed events there as if
they were actually happening.

For the first twenty-five episodes,
Mister Rogers entered singing "What
Would You Like to Do Today?"—a *Children's Corner* song he cowrote with Josie
Carey. Show number 26 introduced a
new opening number, "Won't You Be My
Neighbor?" Fred Rogers entered singing, "It's a beautiful day in this neighborhood," as he would hundreds and hundreds
of times in the years to come. (Despite all

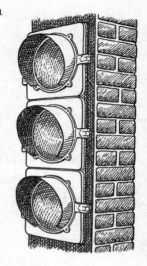

that repetition, the lyric was commonly misheard as "It's a
beautiful day in the neighborhood.")

By February 1967, the show was on the air in eight markets:
Pittsburgh, New York City, Chicago, San Francisco, Philadel-
phia, Boston, Maine, and Schenectady, NY. Los Angeles and
Miami soon followed. The funding, however, was precarious—
from week to week, it was never clear whether the show would
stay on the air.

Josie Carey worked on the show for a few weeks, making her
final appearances on a Fred Rogers program in a dinosaur costume, as the character Emily Brontosaurus. For one episode,
she appeared on camera with a lion cub—which got spooked
and attacked her brontosaurus tail. "Fred jumped in front of
the lion and distracted it," she said. Carey went on to other
local television programs; in the 1970s, she hosted a show in
South Carolina called *Wheee!* for 473 episodes. Years later, she

was rueful that her working relationship with Fred had ended and that her onetime partner had left her behind. At the same time, she recognized the magnitude of what he went on to accomplish. "If we had continued to work together, he would never have gotten to be Mister Rogers," she said quietly. "Because I would have been out front, doing my thing."

"This is my major work in life," Mister Rogers said in the spring of 1967. "I don't want to do anything else. I just hope I can make more programs for educational television. So far, we have a total of one hundred filmed shows, which will run out May 19 and will be repeated next season. I hope by then the money is there to make more and do more."

When word spread that *Misterogers' Neighborhood* was having a budget crunch and might be canceled, mothers mobilized to protest and to go door-to-door, raising funds for the show—shocking public television stations that weren't used to having viewers that passionate about anything they aired. Capitalizing on this grassroots passion, Newell arranged for personal appearances by Mister Rogers in some of the cities where the show was broadcast.

In Boston, for example, Mister Rogers made an April 1967 visit to the studios of WGBH, which expected maybe a few hundred people to show up. Instead, it was a replay of Daniel Striped Tiger's birthday party. The *Boston Globe* reported, "Over six thousand wide-eyed children and their determined parents braved raw winds and a half-mile line to meet television's Misterogers, creating what police said was the biggest Cambridge crunch since the Harvard-Yale game." A Los Angeles visit was just as much of a mob scene.

In Chicago, reports of these crowds caught the eye of Bill

McCurdy, the president of the Sears-Roebuck Foundation. Fred said, "He had been talking with NET [National Educational Television, the forerunner of PBS] about underwriting something, never thinking that they might be interested in children's programming. So he got in touch with Paul Taff [NET's director of children's programs] and said, 'What's this *Neighborhood* program about? I understand it needs funding.'"

Taff enthusiastically brokered an initial grant of $150,000 in September 1967, and signed the *Neighborhood* up for the much larger NET network. Initially, he tried to convince Fred to cut the show back down to fifteen minutes, as a money-saving move, but the gentle minister was adamant: the show needed to be half an hour. Taff relented, and NET found the money to match the Sears grant.

"I did not create Fred Rogers," Taff said. "I just knew what he was doing was right."

Fred Rogers had a plan for a half hour of television that was simple, but so sturdy that it would serve him through hundreds of episodes over the next four decades. He explained, "The opening reality of the show, we deal with the stuff that dreams are made of. And then in the Neighborhood of Make-Believe, we deal with it as if it were a dream. And then when it comes back to me, we deal with the simple interpretation of the dream."

Ideally, that structure wasn't apparent to young viewers, he said. "That all sounds very analytical and it probably doesn't show at all—and that's fine. But at least when I'm writing a script, that's what I think about. Anything can happen in Make-Believe, and we can talk about anything in reality."

Mister Rogers' Neighborhood debuted on February 19, 1968. Versions of the show had been airing in North America for

six years already, and elements of it dated back to April 1955, when Daniel Striped Tiger first popped out of a grandfather clock, but Fred always counted this national broadcast as the show's official beginning. (The title card still read *Misterogers' Neighborhood*—it didn't get changed until the following year, when the program went from black-and-white to color. The title change was made for the most Freddish of reasons: to make it easier on children learning to read.) The affiliation with NET and the Sears-Roebuck Foundation provided each episode with a budget of six thousand dollars: still a pittance when compared to commercial programming. *The Banana Splits Adventure Hour,* for example, the antic Sid and Marty Krofft show about a costumed bubblegum rock band, broadcast Saturday mornings on NBC, cost $150,000 for each episode. Just as important as the money was the NET audience: Mister Rogers was now seen nationwide on more than a hundred public television stations.

Fred asked David Newell to supplement his duties as props master and PR rep by taking a role on the show as the local deliveryman—the guy who would bring those props to Mister Rogers' house. The character was called Mr. McCurdy, in trib- ute to Bill McCurdy, the president of the Sears-Roebuck Foun- dation. Just before filming the premiere, Fred got the word: Bill McCurdy worried that it was unseemly to have his name in the show, since it might look like the price of the founda- tion's largesse. According to Newell, "Fred said, with twenty minutes to go before the taping, 'We have to get you a name.' Seconds later, he blurted out 'McFeely.'" McFeely was Fred Rogers' middle name, but more important, it was the name of his beloved grandfather Ding-Dong, whose unflagging love had buoyed Fred all through his childhood.

In that first episode, Mister Rogers enters his house, takes a sweater from an otherwise empty closet, and then leaves the closet door ajar. He points out the changes in his house, like the new kitchen: "I'm getting used to it. Took me a little while. All weekend long we've been painting." And he also reminds viewers that they're watching a television show, filmed in "this very special studio."

His speech is deliberate and provides lots of opportunities for children to talk back to the screen. He asks how they're doing with tying their shoes; he asks if they know what a ladder is. (The answer: "A ladder helps you go up and down.") And he looks into the camera and assures that one little buckaroo sitting at home, "I like you exactly as you are."

When it's time to visit the Neighborhood of Make-Believe, Mister Rogers gets a call on a can connected to a string, and then unfolds a sofa bed (for reasons not satisfactorily explained) before finding the Neighborhood of Make-Believe through his telescope.

As ever, there's humor with the puppets: when King Friday discovers that a visitor (Joe Negri) hasn't scheduled time with him, he tells him that he needs to make an appointment for an audience. He gets one, for two and two-tenths seconds later, and is then chided for being late.

The tone of the show on its first week of being broadcast nationally was more explicitly political than ever before: when Lady Elaine Fairchilde uses a magic boomerang to teleport Grandpere's replica of the Eiffel Tower to a new location, King Friday gets so agitated that he declares a state of emergency, establishes border guards, and has barricades put up, all to prevent any future changes.

King Friday's niece Lady Aberlin, played by the young human

woman Betty Aberlin, visits to find that her uncle has become a military despot. When he drafts Lady Aberlin into his army, she concocts a plan with Daniel Striped Tiger, inflating balloons with messages attached like LOVE, TENDERNESS, and PEACEFUL CO-EXISTENCE. They send them floating over to King Friday's castle—but the king interprets them as weapons of war and shouts, "Fire the cannons! Man your stations! Paratroopers!"

Lady Aberlin convinces everyone to hold their fire, and when the king discovers that the paratroopers are actually messages of peace, he orders an end to all fighting.

"It *worked,* Daniel," Lady Aberlin tells the anxious tiger.

"I'm so glad," Daniel responds, "because we wanted everybody to have peace, didn't we?"

Those programs aired when the United States was waist-deep in the Vietnam War: three weeks before had come the fierce fighting of the Tet Offensive, when many Americans realized that the North Vietnamese forces were more potent than American leaders had admitted, and that the conflict would not end anytime soon.

Fred Rogers was a pacifist by temperament—but he wasn't rallying preschoolers to march on the Pentagon. He knew all too well that the daily drumbeat of war, in adult conversations and on the evening news, could be terrifying for young children. So he explained war in a way they could understand, he touted peace as an important value, and he gave viewers a sense of control: if kind words and balloons were enough to stop a war, then children might not be powerless themselves. It was a quietly radical message—but even more important to Fred, it was a therapeutic one.

Betty Aberlin was a new addition to the *Neighborhood* ensemble. She had grown up as a "lonely bohemian" in the outer boroughs of New York City; her father returned from World War II but didn't stick around. "We religiously followed the Orthodox Jewish atheism," she said of her unconventional childhood. She started dancing and acting at a young age, and when she was around ten years old, she made her stage debut in *Sandhog,* a folk opera based on a novel by Theodore Dreiser, co-written by Waldo Salt and Earl Robinson, both on the Hollywood blacklist because of the Red Scare. Aberlin remembered that when she did the play, "My mother was asked if she minded that I would be a Communist by association at age ten."

Aberlin went to Bennington College, where she studied writing with the novelist Bernard Malamud; after graduating in 1963, she bounced around the fringes of show business. Quick-witted and beautiful, she helped to start a radio station and joined the road company of *The Mad Show,* a hit musical revue (the branding was borrowed from *Mad* magazine, much like *Mad TV* three decades later). Her big number in that show was called "The Boy From . . ." with music by Mary Rodgers and lyrics, under a pseudonym, by Stephen Sondheim. The song was a comic take on "The Girl from Ipanema," sung by a girl unaware that the boy she adores is homosexual, punctuated by her repeatedly singing the name of his hometown, "Tacarembo la Tumba del Fuego Santa Malipar Zacatecas la Junta del Sol y Cruz."

Fred Rogers caught *The Mad Show* in Pittsburgh and was impressed by the ingénue with comic timing and the ability to sing tongue-twisting lyrics. (She knew who Fred was, because she was friendly with actor Don Francks, who had appeared on *Misterogers* in Canada and did a Fred Rogers song in his nightclub act.) He offered her a job; with *Mister Rogers' Neighborhood* getting picked up by NET, he wanted an actress to interact with the puppets on a regular basis—something he had lacked since he parted ways with Josie Carey, seven years earlier, even if he didn't want to admit it.

"If I had known I was taking her place, I probably wouldn't have taken the job," Aberlin said. But she did take it: "All of a sudden, I'm talking to a little sock puppet!"

Aberlin's warmth and empathy put her at the forefront of the show's human cast. Her interactions with the puppets gave them all a greater sense of reality, but she had a particular rapport with the Daniel Striped Tiger puppet, the most vulnerable of all of them: they would rub noses and say "Ugga-mugga," their special code for "I love you." Aberlin said, "Daniel was my surrogate child, certainly."

In the episode of *Mister Rogers' Neighborhood* that aired June 3, 1968, King Friday is sad because he's lonely, so Lady Aberlin brings him a doll and some custard and sings a song about his emotions, "I'm Missing Someone Badly." In the June 4 episode, Mister Rogers sets up an amplifier in his living room and invites an adolescent friend, Johnny Lively, to play some "teenage music," which provokes an explanation of the word "teenage" and a discussion of how practice helps you learn to do something. The show on June 5 features Mister Rogers singing "The Alphabet Song," taking care of a live cat named Pink Paws, and talking about how it can be hard sometimes to visit a place you don't know.

But early in the morning of June 5, there was a breaking news story: presidential candidate Robert F. Kennedy was shot in Los Angeles, dying the day after. It was only a few months after the assassination of Martin Luther King Jr.; worried that nobody was thinking of how children might handle the news, Fred quickly wrote the script for a special prime-time program.

The show opens without a title: Mister Rogers is sitting in his living room, in a suit. He never changes into a sweater, because this program is aimed at adults. He looks uncomfortable and uncertain of what to do with his hands. While he speaks, he scratches a spot on the wall or twists the petals on a flower.

Mister Rogers talks about the different ways that children can process grief and bad news and offers an array of suggestions of how parents might speak with their own children. His conversation is illustrated with scenes in the Neighborhood of Make-Believe, where Lady Aberlin assures X the Owl that when he has angry thoughts, they don't hurt anybody—only actions do. "That man didn't shoot the other man just by thinking about it," she tells him.

Lady Aberlin visits Daniel Striped Tiger. They play peek-a-boo, and then he gives her a balloon. He asks her to blow it up and then to let the air out; she does so slowly. "Where's all the air that's inside?" he asks her. She explains that it's outside, but he's worried that she might blow all the air out of her body. To demonstrate that she'll be fine, she blows it up again, at which point Daniel asks, "What does 'assassination' mean?"

Taken aback, Lady Aberlin lets the air out of the balloon and says sadly, "Have you heard that word a lot today?"

"Yes," Daniel says in a small voice. "And I didn't know what it meant."

"Well, it means somebody getting killed," she says haltingly, "in a sort of surprise way."

"That's what happened, you know! That man killed that

other man," Daniel tells her. They discuss how everyone's talking about it—Daniel wishes they would talk about something else. Lady Aberlin rubs noses with Daniel as they say "ugga-mugga."

Back in Mister Rogers' home, the host says earnestly, "I've been terribly concerned about the graphic display of violence which the mass media has been showing recently. And I plead for your protection and support of your young children."

Even without the Daniel puppet on his hand, Fred Rogers looks intensely vulnerable. Shattered by the tragic news, he's visibly struggling to remain composed, working hard to bring all his talents to bear on the job of being a helper for the nation's children. "He did the most beautiful script," Betty Aberlin said of that show, marveling at how the balloon was the perfect metaphor to help children understand death. "Fred was able to do what is very hard to do, which is he was able to simplify complicated things."

That gift helped make *Mister Rogers' Neighborhood* a huge hit; in Boston, for example, it soon had more viewers of ages two to eleven than anything else in its time slot, beating out *Superman, Batman, Thunderbird, I Spy, Perry Mason,* and *The Merv Griffin Show.* In *TV Guide,* Mister Rogers was named "the Pied Piper of the TV set"; the magazine said he was "fast becoming Drs. Spock and Doolittle rolled into one." In the spring of 1969, *Mister Rogers' Neighborhood* won a prestigious Peabody Award for excellence in broadcasting.

As if Fred Rogers didn't have enough responsibilities with the show, he also flew around the country at the behest of local public television stations, making personal appearances in front of vast numbers of adoring children. He didn't believe that it was possible to make a meaningful connection with a crowd of thousands, so he insisted on doing a day's worth of fifteen-minute visits with smaller groups. But real life intruded on the Neighborhood, as it seemed to do so often.

Fred said that his greatest challenge as a performer was to walk through the door and sing "It's a beautiful day in this neighborhood" on days when he had sorrow in his life. One of those days came when his father died at age sixty-nine. "I had to go to Miami one hour after my father's funeral because they were having a Mister Rogers day there that they said could not be canceled," Fred said. They had given away tickets for twenty-three different time slots. "And I had to sing 'It's a beautiful day in this neighborhood' for each one of them."

Johnny Costa joined him on the trip as accompanist, and before the day started, Fred told him sadly, "I'll try." Fred remembered, "Before he was playing the music, I just started to bawl." Somehow, he got through all twenty-three performances: what sustained him was knowing that he was helping children, which made him feel "that Dad was in a good place."

Another unexpected disturbance came in the spring of 1969: President Richard Nixon, looking to free up funds that he could devote to the war in Vietnam, wanted to cut the budget of the Corporation for Public Broadcasting (CPB), which was then a brand-new source of national funding for public TV (previously, public television stations had to rely solely on local funds). Nixon's predecessor, Lyndon Johnson, had budgeted twenty million dollars of federal money, and Nixon was hoping to cut that appropriation by at least half.

The person who had the most control over the purse strings was John Pastore, the bulldog senator from Rhode Island, son of an immigrant tailor, the shortest man in the Senate, and the chairman of the Subcommittee on Communication. He was a Democrat, and not totally hostile to public television, but he was also fiscally conservative, and remained unconvinced that twenty million dollars for the CPB would be money well spent.

The subcommittee held two days of hearings, on April 30 and May 1, 1969. Mister Rogers showed up at the request of Hartford Gunn, president of WGBH in Boston, who organized the public-television witnesses. Pastore grew tired of experts droning their way through prepared remarks, and so by the time Fred Rogers' turn came, late on the second day, the senator had told anyone with a prewritten speech to just file it with the committee.

Mister Rogers, his hair neatly slicked back, sat down at the witness table. Holding his typed remarks in his left hand, he said, choosing his words carefully, "Senator Pastore, this is a philosophical statement and would take about ten minutes to read, so I'll not do that. One of the first things that a child learns in a healthy family is trust, and I trust what you have said, that you'll read this. It's very important to me. I care deeply about children."

His voice laced with equal parts exhaustion and sarcasm, Pastore asked, "Will it make you happy if you read it?"

Declining to take the bait, Mister Rogers said, "I'd just like to talk about it, if it's alright." He laid out his broadcasting history and the small budgets he worked with, and then said, "I'm very much concerned, as I know you are, about what's being delivered to our children in this country. And I've worked in the field of child development for six years now, trying to understand the inner needs of children. We deal with such things as the inner dramas of childhood. We don't have to bop somebody over the head to make drama on the screen. We deal with such things as getting a haircut, or the feelings about brothers and sisters, and the kind of anger that arises in simple family situations. And we speak to it constructively."

Despite his sour mood, Pastore was leaning forward, paying attention. "How long of a program is it?" he asked. Informed that it was a half hour, he asked, "Could we get a copy of this so that we can see it?"

"I'd like very much for you to see it," Mister Rogers said sincerely. He then delivered an impromptu version of the Fred Rogers manifesto: "This is what I give. I give an expression of care every day to each child, to help him realize that he is unique. I end the program by saying 'You've made this day a special day, by just your being you. There's no person in the whole world like you, and I like you just the way you are.' And I feel that if we in public television can only make it clear that feelings are mentionable and manageable, we will have done a great service for mental health. I think that it's much more dramatic that two men could be working out their feelings of anger, much more dramatic than showing something of gunfire. I'm constantly concerned about what our children are seeing, and for fifteen years I have tried, in this country and Canada, to present what I feel is a meaningful expression of care."

Mister Rogers paused, hoping that his words were having some impact. "Mentionable and manageable" was a catchphrase of his mentor, Margaret McFarland, but he meant every word of his improvised speech.

"Do you narrate it?" Pastore wanted to know.

"I'm the host, yes. And I do all the puppets and I write all the music and I write all the scripts—"

Pastore interrupted his litany. "Well, I'm supposed to be a pretty tough guy, and this is the first time I've had goose bumps for the last two days."

Sitting next to Mister Rogers, WGBH president Hartford Gunn was grinning broadly: this was going better than he could have dreamed. But Mister Rogers was still kneading his own hands nervously. "Well, I'm grateful, not only for your goose bumps, but for your interest in our kind of communication," he said. He then recited the lyrics to one of his own songs, "What Do You Do with the Mad That You Feel?" The song, about childhood anger management, includes the lyrics "It's great to be able to stop when you've planned a thing that's wrong / And be able to do something else instead, and think this song."

Senator Pastore listened intently and at the end, gushed, "I think it's wonderful." As if he were trying to confirm that the sentiment actually came out of his mouth, he repeated it. "I think it's wonderful. Looks like you just earned the twenty million dollars."

The room burst into applause. The following year, the fully funded CPB would establish PBS (the Public Broadcasting System), which would take over the role of NET—and Hartford Gunn would be its first president. In less than seven minutes, armed only with decency and his own force of will, Fred Rogers had secured the future of public television.

EVERY SINGLE TIME FRED ROGERS BEGAN AN EPISODE OF *MISTER Rogers' Neighborhood,* he had a choice. When he opened the front door and walked into his television living room, he could either turn to the viewer's left and walk down a staircase there or turn to the viewer's right and walk down that staircase. He *always* turned to the viewer's right, like a mouse in a maze that's learned where the cheese is—in fact, most people don't know that turning left was even an option.

The set was built with two equally functional staircases, but Mister Rogers invariably took the one on the right, for a multitude of reasons that reinforced each other: Because that's where the closet with his sweaters was. Because he always tried to stage movement on his show going from left to right, believing that orientation would help children when they began to read. Because his young viewers found that consistency reassuring, the same way they found it satisfying when, after donning his cardigan, he would zip it up to the top and then down just a little bit, to make sure that his microphone wouldn't be muffled. Because *he* found it satisfying: once Fred Rogers had made a correct decision, he tried to keep making it, over and over and over.

"I'm not a character on *Mister Rogers' Neighborhood*," Fred Rogers insisted. "I don't think of my time away from the studio as my 'real' life. What I do in the studio is my real life, and the person on camera is the real me. I think children appreciate having a real person talk with them about feelings that are real to them."

He wasn't a lunatic: he understood the difference between fantasy and reality, and he knew that his daily existence didn't involve klieg lights or makeup. But he strived to remain his real self on TV, and then heighten the presentation around him to make for better programming.

One way he did that was by writing his scripts and then adhering to them. Actors who tried to improvise on the *Neighborhood* set quickly learned that the practice was frowned on:

Fred believed that children were owed the respect of dialogue that was carefully constructed, not concocted on the spur of the moment.

Another way was by recruiting sympathetic collaborators who could help bring his vision to life and make the Neighborhood feel like a place that was truly lived in. David Newell as Mr. McFeely became a regular part of the show, usually saying "Speedy delivery!" and rushing off to his next destination: his accelerated pace made for a good contrast with Mister Rogers' deliberate manner. It turned out that Newell could not ride a bicycle, so when the show needed him to pedal around, he got an oversized tricycle with a wire basket.

Fred remembered and liked guitarist Joe Negri from his thirteen-episode holiday-season run on WTAE. Johnny Costa had the position of musical director well in hand, but Fred cast Negri in two roles: in the real Neighborhood, he was proprietor of Negri's Music Shop, while in the Neighborhood of Make-Believe, he was Handyman Negri, in the service of King Friday XIII. When Fred offered him the handyman role, Negri said, "You gotta be kidding. I can't hammer a nail straight!"

"That's okay," Fred assured him. "It's all pretend."

Negri had played guitar with the Pittsburgh comedy duo Brockett and Barbara (who had written and starred in a series of musical revues), appearing on their album *Out of Folkus*. Fred also hired both Don Brockett and Barbara Russell to appear on the *Neighborhood*. While Russell appeared occasionally—

playing women with eccentric passions, such as lampshades and boomerangs—Brockett became one of the show's iconic characters as Chef Brockett, laboring in his bakery with a large toque hat. He initially baked in silence; once he started speaking, viewers learned he had a distinctive, gravelly voice. Because of a childhood exposure to polio, Brockett walked with a visible limp—the show's first visible representative of people with disabilities.

Pittsburgh had a community of performers who had chosen to settle down in Steel City, variously making a living from radio, TV, theater, and even industrial shows. "People applaud the same way in Pittsburgh as they do in New York," Barbara Russell said. Many of these talented people had decided they valued the sense of community in Pittsburgh more than the possibilities of a career in, say, New York City—which meant that they were already living some of the values of *Mister Rogers' Neighborhood* before Mister Rogers tapped them on the shoulder.

George Hill, the advertising man who had made the department-store sponsorship of *Misterogers* happen in 1964, remained a trusted adviser. He led Fred Rogers to Bob Trow, who had started as a singer but was well-known locally for a wide range of zany characters on the hit *Cordic and Company* morning radio show, including Omicron, a bureaucrat from Venus, and Carmen Monoxide, a taxidermist who ran for president with the slogan "I never made a promise that I kept and I don't intend to start now."

Since Fred had taken the radio out of his car, he was oblivious to the glories of morning drive-time comedy, but he quickly recognized Trow's talent, casting him as Bob Trow, workshop owner and fix-it man; the voice of the puppet Harriett Elizabeth Cow; and the costumed characters Bob Dog (an overexcited but well-meaning dog) and Robert Troll (who spoke in quick-paced gibberish).

Robert Troll was one of many characters Fred Rogers created over the years who didn't speak in English. Grandpere spoke exclusively in French, while the Royal Hula Mouse spoke only Spanish. Henrietta Pussycat gradually expanded her English vocabulary, but her favorite word was always "meow." Sometimes, in pursuit of the fierce urgency of meow, she would carry on an entire conversation using no other words. (Fred paid as close attention to her meow-centric dialogue as he did everything else on the show: revising a script where Henrietta had the line "Meow! Meow new house meow meow new neighbors?" he carefully edited out the first and third meows.) Even the trolley could speak with other creatures in the Neighborhood of Make-Believe, in a language of bells and chimes.

Some of these characters were intended to help children learn a second language—in the case of Robert Troll, his gibberish was meant to help preverbal children watching the show master their *first* language. A 1969 episode where Robert Troll is upset about losing his (magic, invisible) ball suggests why Mister Rogers kept returning to these characters. When King Friday says that he doesn't like the way Robert Troll talks, his consort Queen Sara informs him that "the best way to understand Robert Troll is to understand his feelings." Mister Rogers spent a lifetime communicating with children who had strong emotions but didn't always know how to express them—with these characters, he taught his audience, over and over, to listen to more than words.

Many performers would drop into the Neighborhood for a

season or two, and then move on, playing long-forgotten characters like the nurse Maxine Miller, the mime Jewel Walker, and the fitness coach Willie Saunders. But one performer who stuck around for decades was François Clemmons, the first African American to have a recurring role on a children's TV series.

Clemmons had a spectacular, operatically trained voice, which was how he caught Fred's attention—he was the solo tenor in the choir at Third Presbyterian Church in Pittsburgh, where Joanne Rogers was an alto. Clemmons had grown up with a single mother in Youngstown, Ohio, but he earned a scholarship to Oberlin—where he met Martin Luther King Jr., who told him to "keep on keeping on"—and was studying for his master's degree at Carnegie Mellon when he met the Rogers family.

Fred took an interest in Clemmons, which the young man wasn't sure how to interpret, since it happened so rarely. When Martin Luther King Jr. was assassinated, in April 1968, Clemmons was living a few blocks away from Pittsburgh's Hill district, which was soon engulfed by riots and fires. Fred called Clemmons and insisted on picking him up so he could stay safely at the Rogers house.

"I never had someone express that kind of deep sense of protection for me," Clemmons said, "and that experience drew Fred and me really, really close. I thought, 'Well, this is the real thing right here.'"

A few months later, Fred asked Clemmons to join the cast of the show, playing a police officer. "You have a beautiful voice," he told him, "and I think you could find a positive place here in the Neighborhood."

Clemmons was initially uncertain about the offer. "I grew up in the ghetto. I did not have a positive opinion of police officers. Policemen were siccing police dogs and water hoses on people. And I had a really hard time putting myself in that role. So I was not excited about being Officer Clemmons at all."

He said that Fred, however, "convinced me to try and change the images of policemen." And it was important to him to be a visible black face on television: "I can remember how much I wanted to see another black person."

That representation was real, and meaningful—previously the most prominent black character on the *Neighborhood* was Henrietta Pussycat, whose black fur was sometimes earnestly but awkwardly used by the show as a symbol of racial identity. (Lady Aberlin once sang a song of pride to her: "You are pretty / You are black / You are beautifully dressed, finely curled / Perfectly you are pretty / Elegant, you are black.") Clemmons settled into the role, although he remembered that "my friends used to tease me that I was an officer without a whistle, without a billy club, and without a gun, and that I sang all over the place."

Clemmons' presence was never more meaningful than in an episode that aired in May 1969, thirteen months after the shooting of Martin Luther King Jr. Mister Rogers tells his viewers that on hot days, he likes to cool down by putting his feet in cool water, and goes outside with an inflatable wading pool. Officer Clemmons is nearby, so Mister Rogers invites him to join him.

This seems like a simple gesture of friendship, but it took place in a decade when swimming facilities were segregated by race in a large portion of the country. Only five years earlier, an interracial group had staged a "wade-in" at a whites-only beach in St. Augustine, Florida, only to get attacked by an angry mob. St. Augustine wasn't far from Rollins, which had remained whites-only through Fred's college years—but he could, at least, make sure his own Neighborhood was integrated. In his television front yard, two men sit side by side with their feet in a pool, one set of ankles chocolate brown, the other set Wonder Bread white. It's symbolic, yes—but a powerful symbol of inter-racial friendship, one that could mold young minds.

When they finish paddling, Mister Rogers uses his towel to dry off his friend's feet, a gesture that evokes the biblical passage where Jesus washes the feet of his disciple Peter. "I felt unworthy," Clemmons confessed. "Why did he choose me?"

Clemmons said that while his own biological father and his own stepfather had never told him that they loved him, Fred Rogers did. "He was the first one to say 'I love you,'" Clemmons remembered. "It made a huge impact on me."

He soon discovered, however, that the Neighborhood's diversity didn't extend to his homosexuality. One day, Fred called Clemmons into his office (an office to which he had given the young man a key). He addressed him informally as "Franc," pronounced "France."

"Franc, we've come to love you here in the Neighborhood," Fred told him. "Someone, we're not able to say who, has informed us that you were seen at the local gay bar downtown with a buddy from school. Now, I want you to know, Franc, that if you're gay, it doesn't matter to me at all. Whatever you say and do is fine with me, but if you're going to be on the show, as an important member of the Neighborhood, you can't be 'out' as gay."

Clemmons sobbed as Fred cradled him in his arms.

Many people have wondered whether Fred was gay himself.

His gentle disposition, his artistic nature, his almost complete lack of macho, his friendships with gay men—these are all attributes that play into long-held stereotypes that set gaydar buzzing for many people. In addition, his friend William Hirsch said in 2018 that in private conversation, Fred had placed himself in the center of the Kinsey scale of sexual orientation: "Well, you know, I must be right smack in the middle. Because I have found women attractive, and I have found men attractive."

Fred Rogers was married to Joanne Rogers for over fifty years, and nobody who knew them believes he was ever unfaithful in any way. Fred might well have taken a different path if he had been born in 1958 or 1988 instead of 1928. But in the world we actually live in, Fred Rogers may have been bisexual in orientation, or at least open-minded enough to consider that possibility, but he lived his life as a straight man, and seemed perfectly content with that identity.

Fred Rogers, like all of us, was a product of his time and his environment—but he was better than most of us at reconsidering the cultural prejudices he was raised with. If you take the "smack in the middle" comment at face value, it would seem that on this question, he defined himself by his behavior rather than what was in his heart.

Clemmons, who felt that he was in a position to know, remained convinced that Fred was straight. For her part, Joanne Rogers resented the insinuations that her marriage was phony in some way. "I think Fred had that feminine sensibility," she allowed. "All the men I've chosen to have as friends over the years seem to have that, and I think it's a wonderful quality if you can find that in the person you're going to live with." She emphasized, "It was really a very, very good friendship. I've heard people say that men and women can't be friends and lovers. We really were friends, and I know we were lovers."

Years later, Clemmons said he was sympathetic to his mentor's position, that the show couldn't weather the backlash it would get if accused of promoting homosexuality to young children. "Societal norms were vastly different than what they are right now," he said. While Fred took a public stand against racism, he wasn't willing to fight in the same way for gay rights. So at the suggestion of Fred, and with a hard push from his parents, Clemmons married a woman in 1968. (Unsurprisingly, the marriage didn't last—they split six years later.) The newlyweds relocated to New York City so he could pursue his musical career, although Clemmons returned to Pittsburgh whenever he was needed to shoot episodes of the *Neighborhood*.

On one of his visits back to Pittsburgh, circa 1970, Clemmons was standing in the WQED studios, watching Mister Rogers film the end of an episode, saying, "I like you just the way you are, and you make every day a special day just by being you."

Clemmons said, "I was standing on the other side of the studio, but I swear he was looking into my soul. And I stood there and I looked and I looked and he kept looking at me." When Mister Rogers had finished his take and stepped away from the camera, Clemmons walked up to him and asked, "Fred, were you talking to me?"

The answer: "Franc, I've been talking to you for two years. You finally heard me today."

THE SHOW KEPT INTRODUCING NEW PUPPET CHARACTERS, INcluding Donkey Hodie (a pun on "Don Quixote"), a whole family of Platypuses, and most notably, Queen Sara Saturday. "King Friday thought it would be nice to have a wife, and so Queen Sara came along," Mister Rogers explained. Her name came from his own wife, Sara Joanne Rogers, and when he played the Queen, he channeled Joanne's good humor and level-headed nature.

Two years after the introduction of Queen Sara, there was a royal child, which let the show introduce the concept of pregnancy—to the dismay of some parents, Mister Rogers said. "There are some people who still want their children to think that the stork brings the baby or that the baby grows in a cauliflower patch," he complained. "But children understand a lot better. And I hope that we're helping people to become more honest, therefore, more trustworthy."

When Prince Tuesday was born, a jubilant King Friday XIII threw a party and gave out celebratory gifts to the residents of the Neighborhood of Make-Believe. Henrietta Pussycat received the sunshine; Daniel Striped Tiger got the rainbow; X accepted all the trees in the world. Lady Elaine Fairchilde was unhappy with her present—the Equator—and stole all the party decorations.

One big change off camera came with a milk delivery to the Rogers home. Fred said, "I woke up one morning and here was the milk at the door and my picture was on the milk carton." WQED had cut a promo deal without alerting its star employee. Fred, who detested advertising to children, realized that he didn't control his own likeness. In addition, he was unhappy with the way WQED administrators sucked up the money that his show raised, and then nickel-and-dimed him on using the funds. (For example, they didn't want to pay for the *Neighbor-*

hood to have a color monitor because Fred was color-blind—although plenty of other people working on the production weren't.) So Fred put together a nonprofit corporation, Family Communications, which would do its own fund-raising, produce *Mister Rogers' Neighborhood* and hold its copyrights, and rent the necessary office and studio space from WQED. By the end of 1970, Fred Rogers had stubbornly gained control over his own show.

The negotiations were hard-nosed (in public television terms, anyway). As Leland Hazard, president of WQED, said on his way out of one meeting, "I wonder at what age is it that Fred no longer likes you just the way you are?"

Most years through the mid-1970s, *Mister Rogers' Neighborhood* broadcast sixty-five new episodes a year. Doing that many shows on a tight budget meant that there could be retakes if a line was flubbed or a prop was dropped, but that otherwise the pace of the filming had to be brisk. Betty Aberlin said, "It was so low-budget, in a way, it was as close to live TV as you've got. There was no rehearsal time, so you basically learned your lines and then sometimes you had to do something tricky with a puppet or a prop."

Remarkably, that hectic production schedule never affected the deliberate rhythm of the show itself. Scenes wouldn't cut from one camera angle to another more than twice a minute. Mister Rogers was quite content to take three full minutes to watch the fish tank in his kitchen fill up with water from a garden hose; he was comfortable with long silences. "I think silence is one of the greatest gifts we have," he said.

Mister Rogers was credited with writing every episode of the *Neighborhood,* but because sixty-five shows in a season is a huge number, he actually farmed some of those scripts out to uncredited staff members such as Elizabeth Seamans and Eliot Daley. Their teleplays were carefully vetted by him and Margaret McFarland, but Fred insisted on having his name on them as author, saying that he didn't want children to be confused by the idea that somebody else was putting words in his mouth. While there was some validity to that, it seems hard to imagine that pride wasn't also a factor; the same desire to be seen as the sole creator of *Mister Rogers' Neighborhood* sometimes led him to minimize the contributions of Josie Carey to his work, even publicly dismissing his former collaborator as "the secretary."

The show changed as the years went by: Mister Rogers' living room got a paint job, replacing the brown walls with blue ones. New characters were introduced, such as Chuck "Neighbor" Aber, and even new locations, like a soda shop and Betty's Little Theater. Some of the program's evolution, however, was philosophical.

Mister Rogers had never been anyone's definition of macho: "I'm not John Wayne," he acknowledged, "so consequently for some people I'm not the model for the man in the house." Nevertheless, in its early days, his show had enforced traditional gender roles. His song "I'd Like to Be Just Like Mom and Dad," for example, had one verse for girls ("She knows just how to make the beds / And cook things out of rice") and another verse for boys ("He knows just how to drive the car / And buy the gasoline"). But in fits and starts, the show soon evolved from the norms of Fred's own upbringing. He made a point of using gender-neutral language, showing men as being nurturers, and putting women in positions of authority (most notably, Mayor Maggie of Westwood, the town adjacent to the Neighborhood of Make-Believe, was played by the African American woman Maggie Stewart).

Mister Rogers even refilmed scenes in some old episodes, putting on the same outfit he had worn years earlier and substituting gender-neutral language, believing that the show shouldn't be aired in returns if he couldn't stand behind everything that was in it. He also reshot scenes if he learned that he had shown behavior that could be dangerous, like playing with a laser pointer. And in early episodes Mister Rogers sometimes created intimacy with young viewers by saying things like "you're getting so tall," but he later decided to edit out any dialogue that suggested that he was spying on kids through the television set.

He also more carefully enforced the boundary between reality and Make-Believe. Early on, Mister Rogers had conversations with Picture-Picture, which flashed sentences and questions on its screen as he spoke with it. Mister Rogers also used to talk to Trolley, which expressed itself with its bell language. But after he decided that "magic can happen in Make-Believe—and only in Make-Believe," Mister Rogers filmed new segments to be inserted in the place of those dialogues.

The trolley had replaced the telescope as the symbol of transition to the Neighborhood of Make-Believe—although sometimes Mister Rogers would invoke the power of imagination by getting models of the Make-Believe buildings off the shelves of his kitchen, or even travel to the magical kingdom by mimicking the Neighborhood of Make-Believe with mounds of sand in his sandbox.

Something that remained constant: the show's foundation was his knowledge of child development. Adults, and even older kids, might scoff at a song like "You Can Never Go Down the Drain," but from his time at the Arsenal Family & Children's Center, Fred knew that it addressed a real fear for many young children. He met weekly with Margaret McFarland, who was the show's principal psychological consultant (also on call was Fred's personal psychiatrist, Albert Corrado), taping all their conversations. Once in a while during filming, if he was concerned that he wasn't following the best practices of child development, he consulted with her, making the cast and crew wait with the clock running.

Mister Rogers was happy to explain his approach to anyone who cared to listen. "Children are very concerned with body integrity," he said by way of example. "Many see themselves as balloons of a sort, big bags of blood that if punctured might just all waste away. Underlying the work we do is a very sophisticated understanding of the development of the human personality." He shook his head. "And sometimes people say, 'Oh, you do a kid show.'"

When Fred wanted to have a fire as a plot element on the show, he took his ideas to Dr. McFarland first, as per usual. "She helped me to realize that it was essential to deal with control of fluids before even introducing anything about fire. I learned, for instance, that most children's dreams about fire center around their control of their own body fluids! That's how personal a 'fire' can seem to a child," he said.

So the *Neighborhood* ran a week of shows that featured images of liquids: a waterfall by King Friday's castle, a squirt bottle in the bathtub, an open fire hydrant on a New York City street. Only then did they have a tiny fire on the show, caused by a stove left on in Henrietta Pussycat's home. Fred said, "We didn't show flames, just some smoke; and the fire was put out in half a minute by the Make-Believe fire people."

When the episodes aired, Family Communications got seven phone calls from parents complaining that their children had been extremely frightened by the fire on the show; Fred insisted on taking them all himself. "As gently as I could, I 'interviewed' these parents on the phone. It turned out that every one of them had children with urinary difficulties. I was fascinated," he said. "If I hadn't had the developmental insight, I wouldn't have been able to begin to understand the obvious tie between what was presented on our program and the children's personal developmental concerns dealing with anything related to fire."

EVERYONE ON THE SET OF *MISTER ROGERS' NEIGHBORHOOD* KNEW their jobs. Nick Tallo, the long-term floor manager, said, "We had a four-man crew, and three of us were there for almost the whole time"—meaning the three-decade run of the show. Visitors to the studio were often surprised by the appearance of the crew, who shattered the stereotypes you might expect from the employees hired by a Presbyterian minister for his gentle children's show. Especially Tallo: "My hair was down below my shoulders and I had tattoos all over me. I was very courteous, but I was the last person people were expecting to see, and I guess it blew their minds. In the seventies, people were still afraid of people because of the way they looked." He doesn't need to say that Fred Rogers was untroubled by that particular prejudice.

Arthur Greenwald, who worked on special projects with Family Communications, said, "Bobby Vaughn was Fred's cameraman. When Fred talked to the 'you' at home, he was talking to Bobby's camera. Bobby would be the one who tracked Fred in the opening shot, comes in the door, goes to the closet, sits on the bench, goes to the fish tank. Bobby's always there a half-second ahead of him. A camera in the sixties and seventies was a *truck,* but I don't think in the history of the world Bobby Vaughn ever missed a shot. That was a symbiosis that developed over time: it became second nature as everyone focused on the joint mission of helping children."

Similarly, Johnny Costa knew Mister Rogers well enough that he could time his piano runs to coincide with his friend throwing his shoe from one hand to the other at the beginning of the show. Stationed just off camera—sometimes in the "kitchen" part of the set—Costa provided the accompaniment when anybody sang and sympathetic mood music at other times, often using the transition from one setting to the next as an opportunity to improvise with the other two members of his trio, bassist Carl McVicker and drummer Bobby Rawsthorne, playing variations on the melodies from the previous scene. "What we do isn't simple," Costa said. "Fred always says if it's for the children, it has to be the best we can give."

"Fred was really fun to work with," said puppeteer Bob Brown. He and his wife, Judy Brown, were regular guests on the show for four years, starting in 1972. Fred Rogers had admired a production of *Peter and the Wolf* by the Browns and wanted them to come on the program to show an artistic family at work and to stage more puppet shows. The one condition: although the Browns worked with all types of puppets, on the

Neighborhood they would have to restrict themselves to mari-
onettes (puppets on strings), so there would be no confusion
between their creatures and the characters on the show.

The importance of adhering to the script had been impressed on Brown—which left him unprepared for the moments when Mister Rogers himself would improvise. One of
those times came at the end of a marionette circus routine:
three elephants in tutus do a balletic dance, while a baby elephant tries to fall in step, but can't quite keep up with the big
elephants. (Brown was manipulating the baby elephant.)

The elephants were making their exit, Brown remembered,
when "Fred hops up on the marionette stage and says, 'Wait
a minute. I want to talk to you for a minute.'" Brown was si-
lently freaking out: he hadn't prepared an appropriate voice for
a baby elephant.

"Come hop in my lap," Mister Rogers told the baby elephant;
the marionette complied. Mister Rogers asked the baby elephant if it was feeling sad, and it nodded yes. So Mister Rogers
told the elephant that he knew how difficult it was to be little
and to try to do something grown-up.

"I was so nervous," Brown said. "I don't know what the heck
he's going to say, I've got to come up with a cute voice. Fortunately—I don't know if this was intentional or not—every question that he asked the elephant was a yes or no question, so I
didn't have to do a voice."

(If Mister Rogers' primary concern was not putting Brown
on the spot, he wouldn't have improvised the scene at all. It
seems likely that he related to the elephant the same way that
he would have cared for a distressed child—and knew that
when a child isn't speaking, you don't press them.)

After the scene, when Brown recovered from the stress and watched the playback, he had to salute Mister Rogers' instincts: "It was the most terrific ending to the number, because it was so sweet and it was so sensitive."

In the early years of the show, there would sometimes be an audience of children in the studio, especially for episodes where there was a performance of some type within the program (e.g., a talent show in Betty's Little Theater). Children rarely appeared onscreen for reasons both practical (young performers slow down the pace of a shooting day) and philosophical (Mister Rogers wanted all viewers to be able to imagine themselves in a personal one-on-one neighborly relationship with him, not mediated through the presence of another child).

When Brown was performing a complicated marionette show that required multiple takes, he would ask for there to be no children present—he knew that they would quickly grow bored by the necessary retakes. So, in a child-free studio, Brown was doing his version of "Jack and the Beanstalk" when he tangled a marionette string and said, "Oh, shit."

"Everything stopped dead," Brown reported. "You could hear a pin drop. And I looked up very slowly and Fred's standing there with his arms crossed. I said, 'I am so terribly sorry. It just kind of slipped out—I never ever in a million years would talk like that around kids.'"

Brown thought that would be the end of the faux pas, but "Fred came over and lectured me for the next five minutes. I mean, it wasn't *meant* to be a lecture. He said, 'Oh, that's okay, Bob. We all react to stress in different ways and I know you have to express yourself.' He went on and on—I thought, 'I will *never* make this mistake again. I know he's a minister, but seriously, folks, we're all adults.'"

"In all the years I worked on the show, I never heard Fred swear," Nick Tallo declared. "I heard the *puppets* swear. Lady Elaine, the mischievous puppet, she would come over the wall, look right at the camera, and say 'shit.'" (Fred Rogers, of course, provided the voice of Lady Elaine.)

Arthur Greenwald remembered the night when he drove Fred Rogers and Margaret McFarland from a child-development conference at Yale to the airport in Hartford, Connecticut—and ran out of gas on the way. Greenwald was mortified, but Fred kept reassuring him that everything would be fine, and he shouldn't worry about it. However, they were stranded on a deserted road, and after twenty minutes with no cars passing by in either direction, Greenwald was extremely worried that he would be responsible for them missing their plane back to Pittsburgh.

Finally, a police car drove by; Greenwald flagged it down and explained the situation. Happily, the friendly policeman volunteered to drive McFarland and Mister Rogers to the airport. As they got in the back of the patrol car—leaving Greenwald by the side of the road, still out of gas—Greenwald called out, "Fred, what would Lady Elaine say at a time like this?"

The reply came from the backseat of the police car as it pulled away, in Lady Elaine's raspy tones: "She'd say, 'Oh, shit!'"

Tallo remembered that on the *Neighborhood* set, "There were times when Fred was tired or there was a lull, I would think of the absolute filthiest joke I could think of, and I would tell it to Fred. Most of the time, he got it." Tallo laughed. "If he thought it was funny, he wouldn't repeat it, but if he wanted somebody to hear it, he would call them over and make *me* tell the joke. Which I thought was funny."

Photographer Walt Seng similarly tested the Presbyterian minister's limits one day when he was taking a series of portraits of Mister Rogers, both solo and with his puppets of King Friday XIII and Queen Sara Saturday. (Seng photographed Mister Rogers on a regular basis over the years—one of his later pictures, featuring the icon posing with King Friday, ultimately appeared on a 2018 American postage stamp.)

"I was kind of a wise guy," Seng said. Goofing around between shots, Seng took a pencil and stuck it under King Friday's robes, so the cloth protruded in a phallic fashion. Mister Rogers didn't miss a beat. He just said, "My, King Friday, aren't we feeling amorous this morning?"

"He was very serious," Seng said, "but he had a great sense of humor and he was the nicest guy I ever met. He taught me how to listen when people talk. On a break during shooting one day, we started talking and he *listened.* He makes you talk—and he makes you think about what you're going to say. Conversation is about you, not about him. And that's a little bit uncomfortable, because we're not used to being talked to like that, or listened to like that."

Mister Rogers worked in a mass medium that created the illusion for millions of children that he was speaking directly to them. He regarded that bond as holy, and so when he was approached by children, he would unfailingly get down on one knee and give them the time that they needed. When he was a younger man, he had once approached Audrey Hepburn at a hotel swimming pool and asked if he could take her picture, as other people at the pool were doing. She said, "I'd rather not," which crushed him.

"I think of that every time anybody asks if they can take my picture," Mister Rogers said. "I invariably say, 'Of course!' Maybe that's just because I'm who I am." An avid amateur photographer, he would often turn the tables, asking people if he could take *their* picture—and then sending them a print after he got it developed.

Fred also made sure, throughout his career, to reply to every single letter that he received. When *The Children's Corner* got too popular for him to do that personally, the show recruited local high school students to pick up the slack—which worked out well, except for the time some of them got overwhelmed by the mail and burned a bunch of it. When he started *Misterogers* in Canada, he would spend evenings "sitting around the dining room table with my wife and answering by hand all of the mail that came from the children and families," he said. "Our table would be piled high with letters and drawings, and as soon as we had our boys in their beds, we would work until late at night, answering every one."

Truckloads of letters poured in—by 1975, fifteen thousand letters a year. "It's the quality of the letters, it's the quality of the reaching out that is even more important than the quantity. The things that people want to share with you are stunning," Fred said. "They knew we were a safe place to go."

Children wrote to Mister Rogers asking if he was real, or how to stop being afraid of spiders and monsters, or why wishes don't come true. One blind five-year-old girl told him how worried she got if he didn't announce that he was feeding the fish he kept in his tank—after that, Mister Rogers always tried to narrate his daily feeding of the fish. Whether they sent in a handmade picture or confessed their deepest fears, everyone got a personal letter back, vetted and signed by Mister Rogers. (Often, there would be two letters: one for the child, one for the parents.) He and staffer Hedda Sharapan would come into the office on weekends to handle the mountains of mail. "Sometimes we're two, three months behind," he admitted, "but we still answer every letter that comes."

THERE HAVE BEEN FIFTEEN EGOT WINNERS (PEOPLE WHO HAVE been awarded the Emmy, the Grammy, the Oscar, and the Tony), but only one member of that select club has the additional imprimatur of having appeared on *Mister Rogers' Neighborhood*. That's Rita Moreno, who appeared in 1975 with her husband, Dr. Leonard Gordon, and their young daughter Fernanda; Mister Rogers wanted to spotlight a family where the parents had very different jobs. Moreno was starring in the PBS children's program *The Electric Company* at that time, but she happily ceded the spotlight to her husband, who answered Mister Rogers' questions about his work as a medical doctor.

"He brought things like a stethoscope with him and explained their use," Moreno said. "Fernanda, our daughter, was extremely shy, and a big fan of Fred's. She said nothing: she just leaned against me, like a baby horse, as shy children do with their parents. She was a little chatterbox—but not there."

After the conversation about visits to the doctor's office ended, Moreno sang one of Mister Rogers' songs ("It's You I Like") while he played piano. "Finally, it was almost time to leave," Moreno said. "He turned to Fernanda and said, 'Fernanda, would you like to feed the fish?' She, being very shy, nodded yes. So we all went to the fish tank and I think she stood on a chair and she fed the fish, sprinkled some food into the tank. Never said a word."

It was what Mister Rogers did after they said their goodbyes that truly impressed Moreno. "He turned to the camera and said something like 'Did you notice Fernanda's very shy?' And he's looking into the lens and he says, 'But did you also notice that her mommy and daddy love her very much anyway?' I was absolutely poleaxed. It was not something he planned to say, because he didn't know Fernanda until we visited. And I've never, ever forgotten that. It was a service to thousands of children. It was so kind and thoughtful and sweet and smart."

As it happened, there was another Hollywood star in the studio that day—he just hadn't made a movie yet. Working as an assistant to the floor crew was a young man named Michael Douglas; a few years later, when his acting career took off, he changed his name to avoid confusion with the Oscar winner Michael Douglas and the talk-show host Mike Douglas, and became famous as Michael Keaton.

"He was deceptively funny. So authentic, but also so unusual," Keaton said of Mister Rogers. "I was making, like, $2.25 an hour," he remembered. "When you did his show, you did everything, from pull cable for the cameras, to running the trolley, to dressing up in the black-and-white panda suit for twenty-five bucks."

Keaton added, "What people don't realize is what his crew looked like—they almost all had hair down to their lower backs. One guy just dripped with patchouli and marijuana smoke, worse than Tom Petty. But everyone would do these insane things—and Fred just loved them. And they loved him back."

Mister Rogers said of the crew, "We just had a ball. They were always playing jokes on me." One time during rehearsal, they stuffed paper towels in the toes of his dress shoes, so at the end of the program, when he was changing out of his sneakers and back into his shoes, his shoes didn't fit, much to his confusion (and his delight, once he figured out what had happened).

Another time, Tallo took an inflatable sex doll of a woman, put her in a wedding dress, and then stashed her in the closet that held Mister Rogers' sweaters. "He opened that door and jumped back, and I thought, 'Holy shit, I'm going to get my name in *Time* magazine.'" Fortunately, Mister Rogers did not have a fatal heart attack—he just said, "Oh, Nicky," and then embraced the inflatable bride and, laughing his head off, waltzed around the set with her.

That wasn't the biggest surprise ever to be found in Mister Rogers' closet, though. As Keaton told it, "One day we were taping, and Fred comes in, and starts singing 'It's a beautiful day in this neighborhood, a beautiful day,' puts the shoes down here, goes to hang up the sweater in the closet. And he's singing, and he opens the door—and there's his floor manager, Nick, this big guy with his long goatee, pierced ears, hair all over the place, totally nude, just standing there in the closet. Well, Fred just fell down. It was the most hysterical thing you've ever seen." Keaton concluded, "He was totally cool."

"We were very devoted, because we realized we were not in anything we could quit, somehow. We had stumbled into somebody's mission for children," Betty Aberlin said. "If you're the color yellow in Van Gogh's paintings, you can't quit."

Aberlin revered Fred Rogers as a genius, but that didn't stop her from nursing grievances over the years. They disagreed over public performances of his music that she had arranged. It rankled when she was flirting with a stagehand and he chided her, "Remember who you are and what you stand for." But Aberlin's discontent was rooted in her belief that if each of the characters in the Neighborhood of Make-Believe expressed an aspect of Fred's off-camera personality—X the Owl his adolescent curiosity, Lady Elaine his sense of mischief— then most people overstated the extent to which he resembled the timid Daniel Tiger and understated the parallels with the high-handed King Friday. (One of King Friday's trademarks was expecting that every pronouncement he made should be greeted with a chorus of "Correct as usual, King Friday.")

In 1975, Fred made a decision that, if not as imperious as King Friday's commanding that all his subjects learn to play bass violin, still seemed arbitrary: he was ending production of *Mister Rogers' Neighborhood*. He had long touted 780 episodes as his target for the library of *Neighborhood* episodes that would go into perpetual reruns, enough for a young viewer to watch for three years without encountering a repeat. Now, he decided, 455 episodes in steady rotation on PBS would suffice.

He didn't offer any future plans beyond taking a vacation, or any real reason for the decision: it seems likely that he was simply worn out. He had put in too many eighty-hour workweeks; even his summer vacations were spent writing scripts for the following season's shows.

Family Communications scaled down its operations, and after one last week of shows in 1976, the cast of the *Neighborhood* scattered. Joe Negri hosted local TV shows like *Joe Negri's High School Talent Scene* and taught guitar on the university level. François Clemmons continued singing, frequently playing the role of Sportin' Life in *Porgy and Bess*—a recording he made of the show with the Cleveland Orchestra and Chorus won a Grammy. Betty Aberlin went to Hollywood to be part of *The Smothers Brothers Show*, but as soon as she arrived, the series got canceled.

In 1977, Fred wrote a letter to the staff of Family Communications, acknowledging that the company had gone through a difficult year—the only new show of note they got on the air was a Christmas special that got the old *Neighborhood* gang back together—but also expressing optimism that their work in the coming years would meaningfully contribute to the lives of American families. There was a postscript to the letter, a message of a single word, allegedly from King Friday, that sounded like the title of a lost Funkadelic album: "Slopperydozafanundapuk."

Despite that regal nonsense, Fred had turned his attention to adult programming. In 1978, PBS aired twenty episodes of *Old Friends . . . New Friends*, each of them a half-hour visit with a notable figure, some famous ("Stardust" songwriter Hoagy Carmichael, baseball star Willie Stargell), some obscure (barrio teacher Nancy Acosta, Appalachian woodcarver Edgar Tolson). He was a self-effacing host, letting his subjects speak for themselves as they described their searches for meaning in their own lives—classical pianist Lorin Hollander, for example, held forth for over five minutes before Mister Rogers interjected a question. But while he had interesting instincts as a documentarian looking for uplifting stories, the rhythms of the show were too stately and it failed to find an audience. Fred had often said that the *Neighborhood* let him use all his talents, including music and puppetry—now he was denying himself many of those tools.

The most rewarding part of making *Old Friends . . . New Friends* may have come when Fred traveled to Cuernavaca, Mexico, to profile the Reverend William Wasson, who ran an orphanage that had cared for thousands of children. During his visit, a new boy arrived at the orphanage—his grandmother, who looked after him, had just died.

"He really got to me," Fred said, so much so that he gave the boy his own watch. "It was a watch my grandmother had given me. It meant a lot to me. I had one whole night of struggling with 'should I, should I?' Then I thought, 'Just try and see what kind of freedom you'll get from giving that gift.' It was much more a gift to myself than to the kid because I felt free of time. I never wore a watch again."

He concluded, "I think people can really get hooked on material stuff."

WHEN HIS TWO SONS WERE YOUNG, FRED ROGERS WAS THE MOST warmhearted parent possible—he had essentially spent his life preparing to be the father of small children. But he was somewhat flummoxed when his boys, Jim and John, grew into teenagers in the mid-1970s and their adolescent experiments and transgressions seemed impervious to his kindness and understanding. As teenagers, Jim and John found the limits of their father's patience when they installed grow lamps in the family's basement and cultivated a crop of marijuana. Livid, he made the boys disassemble the facility and destroy the pot.

By 1978, John attended prep school forty miles from Pittsburgh, coming home every night so he could sleep in his own bed. Fred and Joanne's older son, Jim, went to Rollins, his parents' alma mater—but once he got there, he went through his freshman year without writing to them or even returning their phone calls.

"He's flown the coop," Fred said, having a conversation with a *People* reporter that he wasn't ready to have face-to-face with his son.

"It's been a difficult year. There's real hostility," Joanne concurred.

"It's been painful, and it's rough on Jamie," Fred said. "But if we don't allow him to go off and have this time for himself, he'll never come back to the nest."

"Mom and Dad have been nice about this break," Jim conceded. "I'm just trying to get used to being a person, to get along by myself."

It's not easy growing up knowing that your father is possibly America's most beloved figure of caring and rectitude, as Joanne acknowledged. "The kids can feel pride for what their father has accomplished, but also jealousy and resentment," she said. "It's difficult to live with an image. Sometimes I want to do something impulsive, silly, adolescent. But then, for Fred's sake, I say 'Don't do that!'"

Or as John put it years later, "It was difficult to have the second Christ as your dad."

In 1979, Fred Rogers achieved a more modest resurrection than the first Christ: as abruptly as he had ended *Mister Rogers' Neighborhood,* he brought it back to life. He came up with a production schedule that was both more manageable and more ambitious: just fifteen episodes a season (down from sixty-five), now organized into three weeklong themes, sometimes on upbeat subjects like "Friends" and "Music," sometimes on difficult topics like "Conflict" and "Divorce." The show had often carried themes and storylines over from one day to the next, so this wasn't totally unprecedented, but if Fred was going to return to the *Neighborhood,* he wanted to go as deep as the format allowed.

The Sears-Roebuck Foundation happily renewed its funding—airing on over 250 stations, *Mister Rogers' Neighborhood* was now one of the crown jewels of PBS—and the show went forward with a budget of fifty thousand dollars per episode (still austere by commercial TV standards). The first week of shows, on the theme of going to school, aired in late August 1979, preparing viewers who would be attending school for the first time the following week. While filming the episodes, Mister Rogers told a visiting camera crew his fundamental reason for returning to the show: "To help kids realize that there are things of great worth within them."

When David Newell told Fred Rogers about news reports of a child who had hurt himself by jumping off a roof, pretending to be Superman, Fred decided to air a week of episodes on the theme of superheroes, designed to help children distinguish Superman from mild-mannered reporters. New episodes of *Mister Rogers' Neighborhood* began when Fred sat down to hash out ideas with Margaret McFarland and continued with him writing the scripts, in longhand on a legal pad, at the Crooked House in Nantucket during his summer vacation.

Shortly before he started writing the "Superheroes" scripts, Mister Rogers was flying from Los Angeles to Pittsburgh, seated behind a young girl; she was traveling alone, afraid to fly, and resisting all the efforts of the flight attendants to cheer her up. Correctly guessing she might know him from TV, he passed her a note that read, "There are lots of reasons to cry and they're all okay. And I'm sitting right behind you and I'd like to talk with you if you would like to talk."

Discussing her fears, and how her own father was terrified of flying, calmed her down, so Mister Rogers spent the whole trip to Pittsburgh talking to her (and two other children who joined them in nearby empty seats), discussing superheroes. "Their associations were what fascinated me," he said. "After the first talk about certain things on television—the Incredible Hulk, Superman, and Robin, and all this—immediately they started to talk about [the nuclear reactor meltdown at] Three Mile Island, and the earthquakes in California, all kinds of things they had no control over. It gave me the greatest hint, really confirming what I already believed—that we put on the guise of being super in order to try to control things that we otherwise have no control over."

Fred took children seriously, and they repaid the compliment. As he said, "I see a lot of children on the streets, anyplace I go, and they never talk to me in a flippant way."

The first stage of filming the *Neighborhood* was to do the remote pieces. In the case of "Superheroes" week, that meant interviewing the stars of the hit *Incredible Hulk* series on CBS: Lou Ferrigno as the angry green giant and Bill Bixby as his puny human counterpart, Banner, showing that what they did on television wasn't real.

The next stage of filming was a season's worth of segments in the Neighborhood of Make-Believe. With so many homes for so many imaginary characters, the set was much too elaborate to be easily erected and dismantled. WQED's Studio A was the largest studio in Pittsburgh, eighty feet by eighty feet, and the Neighborhood of Make-Believe, fueled by Mister Rogers' creativity, had gradually sprawled across the entire facility.

Fred recalled, "Bob Trow walked in one day and he looked at the whole place set up with the Eiffel Tower and the castle and the factory and the tree and Lady Elaine's Museum-Go-Round and all these fanciful places and he said, 'You know, I remember when this was all farmland.'"

The Make-Believe story line for "Superheroes" week centered on a visiting dinosaur that Daniel is afraid of—Fred made sure to feature dinosaurs because powerless children also revere them as beings of great strength.

The final stage of filming was in "reality": the sets for Mister Rogers' house and other locations in his Neighborhood. During "Superheroes" week that included a visit to Bob Trow's workshop, where he was making wooden blocks—which could easily be knocked over, satisfying for a child looking to establish dominion. On another episode that week, Mister Rogers took viewers to the part of Studio A housing the scale model of the Neighborhood seen at the beginning and end of every episode.

Even children could tower over those buildings, which was one reason Mister Rogers showed the model, but another was that he liked to demystify television production. Periodically, he would have the camera pull back to show that his house was actually a set in a studio, or to show how he made Trolley move with a control panel next to his legs, just off

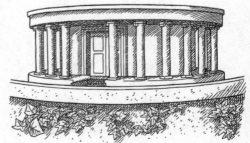

camera: he wanted to be honest with his television neighbors in every way possible.

ANOTHER NOTABLE VISITOR ON THE *NEIGHBORHOOD* WAS LYNN Swann, star wide receiver (and four-time Super Bowl champion) with the Pittsburgh Steelers. He was local, he was happy to talk about safety equipment and uniforms, and as a trained ballet dancer, he could talk about both sports and dance—and perform a quick pas de deux. "The program was straightforward and very engaging," Swann said. "Fred was always Fred. Very thoughtful guy." What Swann didn't expect was how much impact his appearance would make—to this day, he meets people who remember that episode, especially boys who decided it would be okay to try dancing if it was endorsed by a Super Bowl MVP. "It encouraged people to do more things and try more things," Swann said. "The show had a message of understanding."

Another guest who particularly cherished that message of understanding: Ben Adelman, who has cerebral palsy. "He inspired so many people and he made children feel good," Adelman said. In a wheelchair because of his cerebral palsy, he appeared on the *Neighborhood* to show how a wheelchair lift in a van works. But one particular aspect of having a conversation with Mister Rogers made a deep impression on Adelman: "He would look right at you as he was talking to you. A lot of people don't look at me when I'm trying to talk to them."

Big Bird also came to visit, acting as a giant yellow ambassador of the other long-running PBS children's program, *Sesame Street*. Fittingly, his visit was scheduled for the week on "Competition." Mister Rogers initially dismissed that timing as coincidence before allowing, "Well, maybe it was uncon-scious."

To interact with Big Bird, Fred Rogers deployed four of his most famous puppets. Big Bird lopes into the Neighborhood of Make-Believe, carrying a picture he's made of the Neighborhood to enter in King Friday's art contest. X the Owl, excited by the arrival of another bird, has memorized a "welcome poem" and festooned his tree with signs of greeting. All this hullaballoo makes Henrietta Pussycat worried that she's being displaced from X's affections. But she overcomes her jealousy, telling the guileless yellow visitor, "Meow meow meow like you, too, meow Bird!"

The crossover, charming and relaxed, was the product of some heated negotiations. Fred's original script for the show called for Caroll Spinney, the man inside the Big Bird suit, to remove his costume on camera, demystifying it and showing viewers that Big Bird was just a form of dress-up. Spinney refused: he had never done that and didn't want to shatter the illusion of Big Bird. The two men went back and forth on the phone and settled on the compromise that Big Bird would appear only in the Neighborhood of Make-Believe, where the question of his reality would be moot.

Mister Rogers basically got his way, though: he filmed a segment for the same episode where Mr. McFeely delivers an oversized giraffe costume. Before Big Bird shows up, Mister Rogers tries on the giraffe outfit and pointedly tells viewers, "When you see big make-believe creatures in parades or in plays or on television, you know that the people inside are just pretending to be something else."

Fred Rogers respected the honorable intentions of the creators of *Sesame Street* (which made its national public television debut in November 1969—a year and a half after the *Neighborhood,* and just six months after he testified at the Pastore congressional hearings). But he firmly believed that his affective approach, focused on emotional growth, was the superior one for young children, as opposed to *Sesame Street*'s emphasis on cognitive growth, selling letters and numbers with all the whiz-bang techniques of advertising. "I don't think you can separate affective from cognitive learning," Fred said. "Cognitive learning comes about through our being able to receive it—and how can we receive facts except through a comfortable integrative process?"

Sesame Street—dynamic, funny, hip—proved to be the breakout hit for PBS. Its ratings and budgets soon dwarfed the *Neighborhood*'s. Fred claimed that he was happy to have avoided the success of the show he thought of as his program's little brother. Picking his words carefully, he said, "I think that becoming very rich and very famous can be exceedingly seductive. Who knows what would have happened if we had continued to be the only children's program that was national?"

Fred didn't care for most children's TV—but then again, he didn't care for most TV programs. "Television is really part of the extended family now in people's homes," he explained. "It's right in the living room. Young children don't really know if the family approves or disapproves of what is on that piece of furniture. All they know is that mother and father bought it, brought it in there, and set it in the middle of the living room. And how are they to know that it really does or doesn't reflect the family tradition?" He was horrified by *Teletubbies*—that toddlers were watching a show where TV screens were actually integrated into the lead characters' bodies was anathema to him.

While working at NBC in New York, Fred had seen some episodes of Burr Tillstrom's pioneering children's program *Kukla, Fran and Ollie* and was duly impressed—Tillstrom's whimsical, creative use of puppets anticipated much of Fred's own work. And he became good friends with another gentle spirit: Bob Keeshan, better known as Captain Kangaroo.

Captain Kangaroo ran on CBS for twenty-nine years, from 1955 to 1984, and was the closest thing to a commercial-TV version of *Mister Rogers' Neighborhood*. Mister Rogers gave Keeshan one of his highest compliments: "He is a great advocate for children." The two hosts helped each other out behind the scenes—and every New Year's Day, they started the year by getting on the phone and catching up on each other's lives.

One of Fred's pet ideas was that anyone who made or hosted children's programs should undergo specialized training before they were allowed to go to work. "We'd never think of putting anybody on the air to do the news who didn't know how to pronounce 'Vietnam,'" he observed. "But we put on the most important programming, as far as I'm concerned, with people who don't know what their audience is really dealing with."

The Rogers-Kangaroo Institute for Children's Television Programming never opened its doors for business, but Fred reached out to new generations of children's TV hosts on PBS and invited them to appear on his show, so at least they could see how he ran his operation. One of them was Bill Nye, the host of the program *Bill Nye the Science Guy*, who visited the Neighborhood to do an on-air experiment where he blew up a balloon with the chemical reaction between vinegar and baking soda. "It's cool," Nye said. "Literally cool—it's endothermic."

Nye was particularly impressed that when he landed at the Pittsburgh airport, he was picked up by David Newell. "Freaking Mr. McFeely!" he said. "It's a real family operation." Nye was too old to have grown up with Mister Rogers, but he "studied his moves" (and the moves of Don Herbert, host of the long-running TV science-education series *Watch Mr. Wizard*). "The *Science Guy* show was the inverse of the *Mister Rogers' Neighborhood* show," Nye said. "We were fast-paced and frantic, but any show like that has to be an extension of the person on camera or it's not going to work." But he tried to emulate the core feeling of the Neighborhood, especially when he was explaining germs and HIV, knowing that the topic could be scary for young viewers: "When you watched Fred Rogers, you had the feeling that this guy cared about you. I really tried to bring that to all my performances on the *Science Guy* show."

LeVar Burton, who hosted *Reading Rainbow* for twenty-three years, beginning in 1983, first met Fred Rogers at a PBS cocktail party in Crystal City, Virginia. "I didn't grow up watching Fred, but I was certainly familiar with him, and I was intensely interested in meeting the real man," Burton said. "Which is to say, I wanted to know what he was like when he wasn't on camera, because I was certain that was an act. And it soon dawned on me: that was his authentic self. He was that genuine, he was that compassionate, he was that present." Burton had studied for the Catholic priesthood as a young man; Rogers became not only his colleague, but his friend and mentor.

"I think the most important and impactful advice I ever got from Fred was the notion that it was okay to use TV as a medium of message and ministry," Burton remembered. "There was no conflict in using a very secular medium for a holy purpose."

For many years, the Burton family and the Rogers family met at Walt Disney World around Christmastime: Fred and Joanne both loved Disney's Candelight Processional, which told the Nativity story with a fifty-piece orchestra. "We'd meet backstage at the concert—we didn't tour the park together," Burton said, although he enjoyed the mental image of Mister Rogers riding roller coasters in the Magic Kingdom.

"It's not always what he said," Burton observed. "For most of us, when we think of Fred, it's how he made us feel. I know that's true for me. He made me feel seen; he made me feel important; he made me feel loved. That's what I remember about Fred. And that twinkle in his eye."

Knowing exactly how to talk to his audience, Mister Rogers continued to lay out the themes of his shows methodically. In every episode, ideas were introduced, discussed, and recapped, in a way that some adults found maddening but most children found comforting. He did weeks of programs on "The Environment," "Nighttime," and "Imaginary Friends," without much notice outside the day-care demographic—but a week of episodes on "Conflict" got a lot of attention, because they aired in November 1983, coincidentally the same week as ABC's drama about a nuclear war, *The Day After*.

The shows were a reprise of the plot from the first week of nationally televised *Neighborhood* episodes: fearing that the nearby community of Southwood is stockpiling weapons for war, King Friday XIII militarizes the Neighborhood of Make-Believe. By the end of the week, he discovers that it's all a terrible mistake: Southwood is building a bridge, not weapons.

Mister Rogers introduced his viewers to realpolitik and international diplomacy in an age-appropriate way, telling them, "Rules are very, very important. Not just for games but for all things. Even big things like countries. Countries have to have rules to protect people, too. And someday you'll be helping to make the rules for your country. I trust that you'll make the best kind you know how."

The week ends, unusually, with a written message on the screen:

And they shall beat their swords into plowshares;
And their spears into pruning forks;
Nation shall not lift up sword against nation;
Neither shall they learn war any more.

The source was Isaiah 2:4; quoting a biblical passage was the most overtly religious the program had been in some years. The young man who had once threatened to walk out if NBC didn't let him perform "Goodnight, God" had grown into somebody who took the underlying purpose of his televised ministry very seriously but didn't want to alienate any viewers who might be open to its message. He said, "It scares me if somebody should say 'This is a church service' or 'This is a synagogue service' or 'This is a Knights Templar service' or this is any kind of service, because in so doing there are some people who would feel excluded, and I just don't like that."

Nevertheless, his faith deepened as the years went by. Fred Rogers went to bed every night at 9:30 P.M. so he could wake up at 5 A.M. for prayers, Bible reading, and uninterrupted, quiet reflection. The prayers included a long litany of the family and friends whom he loved; he prayed for their well-being and for himself to be mindful of their presences in his life.

He had a simple breakfast every morning: granola with bananas on top and skim milk. Instead of coffee or tea, he drank hot cranberry juice. "I just warm the juice up in the microwave," he said.

(Lunch was typically some combination of yogurt, cheese, and wheat crackers. His favorite beverage was water with a slice of lemon. Dinner was pasta, usually angel hair, "plus vegetables and lentil burgers." No meat: "I was a vegetarian long before it was fashionable," he said. "I just don't eat anything that had a mother, that's all." Fred and Joanne almost always had dinner together, just the two of them. He said, "She herself will tell you that she's not a great cook, but we've found all kinds of frozen stuff that we like.")

After breakfast, he would head over to the Pittsburgh Athletic Association for his morning swim. Every morning, Fred Rogers weighed himself at the gym, and almost every day, the scale said the same thing: 143 pounds. On his six-foot frame, that was a lean weight, a daily reminder of how far he had come since the days when other children tormented him by calling him "Fat Freddy." But the number seemed more profound than that to Fred: he interpreted "143" as a daily affirmation from the universe, a reward for his rituals and routines.

"The number 143 means 'I love you,'" he explained. "It takes one letter to say 'I' and four letters to say 'love' and three letters to say 'you.' One hundred and forty-three: 'I love you.' Isn't that wonderful?"

Another daily prayer came just before Fred got in the water: he would sing, quietly but audibly, "Jubilate Deo," a song his friend Henri Nouwen learned from the Taizé monastic community in France: "Jubilate Deo, jubilate Deo, alleluia." ("Rejoice in the Lord, rejoice in the Lord, hallelujah.") Then, in trunks and swim cap, Fred would swim for a half mile and emerge from the pool feeling cleansed and baptized.

"I like people to tell me if there's something I can do that's better than what I'm doing," he said—even after decades in the pool, he was modest about his technique. "One of the guards is so generous with his knowledge of swimming. He told me, 'You're wasting a lot of energy on your backstroke.'" When Fred asked how he could correct that, the lifeguard told him to keep his feet under the water while he kicked, avoiding the excess effort of splashing. The advice proved to be spot on and true to Fred's principles: he always wanted to get as much done as possible with the least amount of froth.

After his swim, Fred headed to the Family Communications offices at WQED, driving one of a series of unassuming vehicles. Circa 1988, it was a black Oldsmobile that he had bought from John Costa Jr., the son of his musical director Johnny Costa. Fred didn't haggle with him: "I knew John would give me the best possible price," he said. (Fred was handsomely paid by public-television standards—by the end of his career, he received an annual salary of $139,000 from Family Communications—but could have made much more in commercial television, either as a star or as an executive.)

Family Communications had a staff of sixteen people in this era, many of whom stayed there for decades, acolytes of both Fred Rogers and his mission. Fred once asked, "You know how when you find somebody who you know is in touch with the truth, how you want to be in the presence of that person?" He was talking about his spiritual teachers, theologians like William Orr and Henri Nouwen, but it succinctly explained why his staff had such low turnover.

Fred Rogers had a corner office at Family Communications, but it wasn't lavish; he occupied a cozy room with a view of the WQED parking lot. It was filled with soft colors and objects that had personal significance for him: A map of Nantucket, rendered in needlepoint by his mother. A wooden plaque with the single word "χάρις"—Greek for "grace." Drawings by children from around the country, taped to the walls. A Hebrew passage: the portion of the Song of Songs that translates as "I am my beloved and my beloved is mine." At the door, umbrella stands made from plaster casts, the remnants of an ankle injury Fred suffered: a daily reminder of his own human frailty. A huge oil painting of a kid with a fishing pole.

"Oh, that kid is *sooo* many things in me," Fred said, explaining the significance: "He has a fish, which not only symbolizes a Christian faith, but the love I felt for my grandparents. When I was growing up, one of my grandfathers regularly took me fishing, while the other always wanted to take me deep-sea fishing. But he didn't get to. He died when I was a child."

The battered gold paisley couches in the office, which looked as if they had been reclaimed from the Salvation Army, were another reminder of family: they were hand-me-downs from Grandfather McFeely, aka Ding-Dong, who nurtured young Fred Rogers (and took him fishing). If you walked into the office, you would find Fred, usually dressed more formally than he was on-screen: in a pinstriped suit, he looked more like a mortgage broker than a TV host. Surrounded by piles of toys he was supposed to autograph for children, a stack of yellow legal pads, and two cans of teal Flair felt-tip pens, he would usually be reclining in a high-back leather armchair, writing a script on one of the legal pads. "There was never a time when he wasn't thinking and writing about children, and rewriting, and revising," said his colleague Arthur Greenwald.

The most important object in the office to Fred was probably a framed quotation from Antoine de Saint-Exupéry, pilot, aristocrat, dashing war hero, and author of the classic 1943 novel *The Little Prince*: "*L'essential est invisible pour les yeux*," which means "What is essential is invisible to the eyes."

"Those may seem like unexpected words in the office of a person who works in such a visual medium as television," he said, "but I find the truth of those words growing deeper within me every day."

The quotation, essential for anybody spending time with Fred Rogers, wasn't just a message that any child's inner life was an awe-inspiring landscape vaster than most adults could ever imagine. It expressed one of his fundamental beliefs: the moments that gave meaning to life were infused with the Holy Spirit, the presence of God ineffably binding together the universe. They rarely flickered into human awareness, but he knew it happened when two people found a secret bond by praying for each other, or when Johnny Costa's music elevated all the mundane efforts of filming a television show, or when Mister Rogers helped a four-year-old child lying on a shag carpet thousands of miles away, watching his show.

Here are some things Fred didn't keep in his office: his various awards and honors (for a while, they got stashed, in a haphazard fashion, on top of a filing cabinet in the hallway outside his office). A computer. And most notably, a desk. He made room for a piano, but when he had visitors in his office, he didn't want a large piece of furniture in the way of their conversation, casting him as the authority figure and them as supplicants. A friend described the office as "a teddy bear's den made mostly for listening."

Fred Rogers' greatest talent may have been that he was an excellent listener. When Jay O'Callahan was beginning a new career as a professional storyteller, he was booked on the *Neighborhood* and given five minutes to relate a fairy tale he had invented to entertain his children on a long drive to Nova Scotia, about a king trapped inside a bubble. The performance took place on the sidewalk just outside the front door of Mister Rogers' television house. The camera stayed locked on O'Callahan as he talked. Mister Rogers sat on the porch the whole time, giving O'Callahan his rapt attention—even though he wasn't in the camera's frame, he was determined to be the best possible audience.

The summer before, Fred had invited O'Callahan to visit him in Nantucket to discuss his appearance. Fred met him at the airport and drove him to the Crooked House, where he made tea. "I felt like a guest, and it was so relaxed," O'Callahan said. On the way to the house, on the western tip of the island, Fred picked up a teenage boy who was hitchhiking, surprising and impressing O'Callahan. But Fred not only gave the boy a ride, he made sure to include him in the conversation, asking him whether he preferred boating or swimming. Fred ignored class hierarchies with the blithe assurance of somebody who had grown up as the richest kid in town.

Although there was no studio audience per se in the later

years of the *Neighborhood,* frequently there were young visitors: often, terminally ill children who watched a day of filming by the graces of the Make-A-Wish Foundation or another charitable group. They would be warned ahead of time that Mister Rogers would be busy filming the show, but as always seemed to happen when there were children in the room, he would end up giving them his full attention.

When Mister Rogers was booked as a guest on *The Oprah Winfrey Show* in 1985, he specifically requested that there not be any children in the audience—he knew that if there were, he would end up focusing on them and their needs instead of giving a good interview. The *Oprah* producers salted the audience with families and kids anyway, and although Mister Rogers offered a few adult-friendly sound bites—that to connect with children, "I think the best that we can do is think about what it was like for us"—Winfrey soon found that she had lost control of her own program, as Mister Rogers gave hugs and ministered directly to his youthful congregation.

When a group of children visited the *Neighborhood* studio one day in 1989, they delighted in exploring the set: checking out all the famous sweaters in the closet; opening the fridge in the kitchen to discover a plastic head of lettuce; going in and out through the front door, back and forth, over and over, toggling between the Neighborhood and the outside world, getting a small taste of the power of Mister Rogers. When one of them shyly walked up to the host on a break in the filming, Mister Rogers immediately crouched down so he could make eye contact and extended his right hand. When the child hesitantly took it, Mister Rogers said, "You are so brave to shake my hand"—and then they smiled at each other.

Fred Rogers told the writer Tom Junod about a trip he took to California, where he met with a fourteen-year-old boy with cerebral palsy. Because of the boy's condition, he didn't have the motor control needed to speak (he communicated through a computer) and when he was younger, some of his caretakers had abused him. He grew up loathing himself, convinced that God must hate him to punish him so, and sometimes even balling his hands into fists and punching himself as hard as he could. But he had loved *Mister Rogers' Neighborhood* his entire life, and so when he heard Mister Rogers was going to visit him—a charity made the arrangements—he was thrilled and terrified.

When Mister Rogers arrived, the boy was so nervous, he kept hitting himself, badly enough that his mother took him to another room to calm him down. When he returned, Mister Rogers talked to him, quietly and patiently, and then he had a question for the boy: "I would like you to do something for me. Would you do something for me?"

The answer was yes: *of course* he would do anything Mister Rogers asked of him.

Mister Rogers said, "I would like you to pray for me. Would you pray for me?"

The boy fell silent, which meant that his computer fell silent as well. He had no idea what to say—nobody had ever asked him for anything like this. Junod wrote, "The boy had always been the *object* of prayer, and now he was being asked to pray for Mister Rogers, and although at first he didn't know if he could do it, he said he would, he said he'd try, and ever since then he keeps Mister Rogers in his prayers and doesn't talk about wanting to die anymore, because he figures Mister Rogers is close to God, and if Mister Rogers likes him, that must mean God likes him, too."

Junod praised Fred for being perceptive and clever in finding a way to reach the soul of the damaged boy. Fred was perplexed; he couldn't quite believe that Junod had misunderstood him so. "Oh, heavens, no, Tom!" he said. "I didn't ask for his prayers for *him;* I asked for me. I asked him because I think that anyone who has gone through challenges like that must be very close to God. I asked him because I wanted his *intercession.*"

When you walk a mile in Mister Rogers' sneakers, the world looks like a different place. It is not so important who receives the gift and who gives it.

WHEN FRED ROGERS LOOKED INTO THE CAMERA, HE WAS THINKing of one little buckaroo, but the person he saw was floor manager Nick Tallo, complete with beard, ponytail, earring, tattoos, and wardrobe of black T-shirts, some of them from sex-toy shops. Tallo would put his face as close to the camera as possible so he could encourage the man wearing the sweater. "If he looks uncertain," Tallo said, "I'll smile so he knows everything's okay."

Speaking of the people who worked on the *Neighborhood*, Tallo said, "It was real tight—we were a family." He would sometimes take time off from WQED to go work on other jobs— two or three months on a feature film could mean some serious money—but "it got to the point where I wasn't allowed to be off if they were shooting Rogers. I took a commercial and I was gone for two days and they got this other kid to be floor manager and it was a mess."

Mister Rogers didn't chew out the tyro—that was never his way—but those who knew him well had no trouble understanding his displeasure. Tallo and Mister Rogers had a shorthand from their years together that helped the show run smoothly: "If something was wrong, Fred would make a face and I'd know something had to be taken care of."

After he filmed a scene, Mister Rogers would watch the take on the studio monitor to make sure it was up to his standards: clear, good posture, appropriate pace. One day he told a visitor, "The trick is to do it quickly and make it seem like it's really slow."

"That's what I try to do with sex," one member of the floor crew wisecracked. Everyone laughed good-naturedly; Mister Rogers smiled, shook his head, and covered his face with one hand. Tallo, quick to reassure him, gave him a hug. "That's okay, Freddy," he told him.

"Fred was clueless," Tallo said affectionately. "Freddy was the rich kid who lived in the big house and we were the crazy kids who lived in the alley." If Mister Rogers ever had to demonstrate something on camera involving a tool, Tallo and another crew member would sit down with him at the kitchen table on the set and teach him how to use it. "Fred had no idea what they were for, but he would learn," Tallo said.

The unlikely bond between Nick Tallo and Fred Rogers grew stronger as the years went by. "Not to brag, but Freddy was one of my best friends," Tallo said. Sometimes, if Tallo was going through hard times, the phone would ring at home— exactly when he needed to hear a kind word, Fred would call to offer counsel and friendship. After he hung up the phone,

Tallo would say to himself, "I'll be goddamned. That was Fred Rogers."

During breaks in the shooting day, "every once in a while, we would sit down and just bullshit," Tallo said. "He called me over one day and told me that his two boys, their grandmother wants to give them each ten thousand dollars. But Johnny, the younger one, wants to buy something called a Trans Am. He asks, 'What's a Trans Am?'"

Tallo said, "'Fred, it's a hot rod that can go two hundred miles an hour. You don't want him to buy that—he'll end up dead or in jail.' And of course, the kid bought the car and he got in trouble.

"That's the most fulfilling job I've ever had in my life—I learned so much from Freddy about kids and people," Tallo said. "I don't think I've ever met anybody else in my entire life who was as genuine as Fred. He was a wonderful man. He made me want to be a better person."

Does he miss him?

"Every day of my life."

THE YEARS WENT BY; GENERATIONS OF CHILDREN WATCHED *MISTER Rogers' Neighborhood* and then moved on from the show around the time they entered elementary school. But even when they developed adult tastes, for punk rock and sarcasm and post-modern fiction, the love Mister Rogers had shown them could sustain them for a lifetime, although they might no longer re-member the details, beyond a vague nostalgia for trolleys. The *Neighborhood* was on the air so long that some of those children grew up to have children of their own, and entrusted them to the care of Mister Rogers five days a week. Enough time passed that Mister Rogers' hair turned gray and he started attending funerals for members of the *Neighborhood* family.

Don Brockett, who had played Chef Brockett, died in 1995. Johnny Costa, the indispensable musical director, died in 1996. Bob Trow, who had played Bob Dog, Robert Troll, and Harriett Elizabeth Cow, died in 1998.

Fred keenly felt those losses and wearied of the makeup and the contact lenses he had to wear when he filmed episodes—he found them uncomfortable and, in a small way, dishonest. In his bones, Fred knew it was time to end the *Neighborhood*. He made a plan to wind down production (slowly, out of consideration to the people employed by the show and Family Communications): there would be just ten episodes of *Mister Rogers' Neighborhood* airing in 2000, and then a final five in 2001.

Mister Rogers received a steady stream of honors as he walked toward the finish line: a star on the Hollywood Walk of Fame, a lifetime achievement Emmy, a Presidential Medal of Freedom. He gave commencement addresses and received honorary degrees—so many of them that he took all the ceremonial hoods that came along with the diplomas, and stitched them into a quilt. And then he kept getting degrees, and made a second quilt.

The final episode of *Mister Rogers' Neighborhood* wasn't a grand finale that wrapped up long-running plotlines or resolved the show's mysteries (why didn't Daniel Striped Tiger's clock have hands on it?) or even said goodbye. The last episodes were designed to go into rotation with the rest of the show's library: after thirty-three years on the air, Mister Rogers hoped he had made a classic that would live on in reruns for another thirty-three years. (Technology outpaced that desire—the show is now primarily available on DVD and via streaming video.)

There were valedictory notes—when François Clemmons made his final appearance, Mister Rogers reprised their most famous scene together from 1969, once more filling up a wading pool so they could dangle their feet in it together, enjoying the pleasures of cool water and an old friendship. When Mr. McFeely made one last delivery, Mister Rogers formally shook his hand. In the last day in the Neighborhood of Make-Believe, Lady Elaine Fairchilde judged an arts contest and awarded first-place prizes to everyone. The final song Fred Rogers sang on his show was "I'm Proud of You."

On August 31, 2001, the final episode of *Mister Rogers' Neighborhood* aired on the PBS network. Less than two weeks later, terrorists hijacked four planes and crashed three of them into the World Trade Center and the Pentagon, killing thousands of people and terrifying adults and children alike.

Thirty-three years earlier, Mister Rogers had filmed a half-hour program where he gave parents suggestions on how they might discuss a spate of political assassinations with their children. Now, with the nation once more in turmoil, he did what he could to help. Sitting at a piano in front of King Friday's castle, he made a video that distilled what he knew into less than a minute: When children ask about scary events, find out what they already know, because their fantasies may be worse than the truth. Looking straight into the camera, Mister Rogers said, "What children probably need to hear most from us adults is that they can talk with us about anything and that we will do all we can to keep them safe in any scary time."

Fred Rogers kept busy at Family Communications. Television had been his primary medium, but he had always communicated his beliefs through any means available to him: books, record albums, conversations with hitchhikers. Now he helped plan the Fred Rogers Center at St. Vincent's College, in his hometown of Latrobe, hoping that would be the locus of his work in retirement.

Fred had, however, been suffering from stomach pain for some years. He put off going to the doctor, both because he was busy and because, with his regular exercise and abstemious diet, he thought of himself as a healthy person. The pain steadily grew worse, becoming bad enough that he got a thorough examination in October 2002. The cruel diagnosis: stomach cancer.

Even after that news, Fred delayed treatment, not wanting to cancel his personal appearance as a grand marshal of the Rose Parade on the first day of 2003. He made it through the parade, riding through the streets of Pasadena, California, on the same float as Bill Cosby, holding Cosby's leg so he could remain upright. Cosby later said that Fred had gripped him so tightly, his leg was bruised.

A hospital visit was scheduled, with the goal of arresting the cancer by removing half of Fred's stomach. That was not to be: surgery revealed that his body was riddled with cancer. The surgeons removed his whole stomach and sent him home for his final days.

When Fred woke up in the middle of the night, he would

read the books on religion and theology he kept by his bedside. He arranged for gifts to be sent posthumously to people he cared about. He worried about how his family would manage without him. And in his final hours, he asked Joanne, "Am I a sheep?"

The reference was to one of the teachings of Christ (Matthew 25:31–46): when the final judgment comes, Jesus Christ will separate humanity like sheep from goats, taking the former into his heavenly embrace and consigning the latter to eternal torment. Sheep, according to Christ, are those who helped people in need: "I was hungry and you gave me food, I was thirsty and you gave me something to drink, I was a stranger and you welcomed me, I was naked and you gave me clothing, I was in prison and you visited me."

Fred Rogers didn't ask "Was I a good person?" or "Will I go to heaven?" He asked something more theologically specific: *Did I offer succor to the lowliest members of society?* Even after a lifetime dedicated to caring for the powerless, he doubted that he had done enough.

"If anyone is a sheep, you are," Joanne assured him.

In the company of loved ones in his own home, Fred Rogers died on February 27, 2004. He was seventy-four years old. He left behind a visible legacy (television programs, books, Daniel Tiger puppets) that was dwarfed by his invisible legacy: the lives he had made better, the inspiration he had provided to children and adults, the care he had given to people he knew and people he didn't. And there was one final message. At the same time Fred Rogers recorded that PSA about helping children process public traumas, he recorded a few words (carefully chosen, as always) for everyone who had grown up watching his program. As the camera slowly zoomed in, he said goodbye.

I'm just so proud of all of you who have grown up with us. And I know how tough it is some days to look with hope and confidence on the months and years ahead. But I would like to tell you what I often told you when you were much younger: I like you just the way you are.

And what's more, I'm so grateful to you for helping the children in your life to know you'll do everything you can to keep them safe and to help them express their feelings in ways that will bring healing to many different neighborhoods. It's such a good feeling to know that we're lifelong friends.

PART II

Ten Ways to Live More Like Mister Rogers Right Now

Be deep and simple.

When Fred Rogers was in the seminary, preparing for life as a Presbyterian minister, he would attend the sermons of as many different preachers as he could, learning the various ways that a homily could move the soul. Circa 1958, on a weekend vacation in a small New England town, Fred and some friends decided to visit the hamlet's chapel, having heard that the local preacher was impressive.

Unfortunately, in the pulpit that Sunday was an aged substitute, filling in for the absent minister. "I heard the worst sermon I could ever have imagined," Fred remembered. He sat in the pew, quietly wincing, itemizing all the ways the substitute was violating the homiletic rules that the seminary had been teaching him.

The pinch-hitting preacher finally—"Mercifully," Fred said—ended and Fred turned to the woman sitting next to him. To his surprise, his friend had not been enduring the sermon while grinding her teeth: she had tears running down her cheeks.

"He said exactly what I needed to hear," she whispered.

Fred was stunned for a moment, but then had an epiphany. "The woman beside me had come in need," he said. "Somehow the words of that poorly crafted sermon had been translated into a message that spoke to her heart. On the other hand, I had come in judgment, and I heard nothing but the faults."

Thunderstruck, Fred resolved to learn from the experience: "That sermon's effect on the person beside me," he said, "turned out to be one of the great lessons of my life." If somebody didn't hear what Fred was saying, then it didn't matter whether it was because it was poorly expressed or rejected out of hand; Fred would need to find another way to say it, and then another, and hope that eventually his message got through. Conversely, if somebody wanted to hear what he was telling them, he needed to make the most of that opportunity. Fred said, "I now know the space between a person doing his or her best to deliver a message of good news and the needy listener is holy ground."

Working to consecrate the speaker-listener union, Fred Rogers constantly searched for new ways to express his beliefs stripped of any rhetorical flourishes. He rarely quoted from scripture, but Biblical passages could inspire him to write a song or a sentence. He was a master at boiling down both theology and the wisdom of child development into concise messages that could touch people's lives.

Consider this passage by Fred Rogers: "How our words are understood doesn't depend just on how we express our ideas. It also depends on how someone receives what we're saying. I think the most important part about communicating is the listening we do beforehand. When we can truly respect what someone brings to what we're offering, it makes the communication all the more meaningful."

That's a succinct paragraph containing much wisdom about how people can better communicate. If, however, you ironically hear it as "blah blah blah communication" (or "meow meow meow communication"), Fred Rogers can offer you a similar sentiment in two poetic lines: "We speak with more than our mouths. We listen with more than our ears."

Always speaking from the heart, and always looking for the best way to share his beliefs, Fred summarized the approach that worked best for him as "deep and simple." He treasured books on theology by the likes of Henri Nouwen, Gerald May, and Anne Lamott, and he could speak learnedly on eschatological principles, but the books of philosophy he wrote himself were collections of aphorisms, featuring advice such as "Try your best to make goodness attractive. That's one of the toughest assignments you'll ever be given."

Fred Rogers wanted to distill the hard-won truths from his years of life and study, reducing them to their essence. That was a habit born from communicating with children, but he learned that it was also the most effective way to inspire adults to be the best versions of themselves. That approach could slice through the complexities of the modern world like Alexander the Great cutting the Gordian knot. And it penetrated the intricately tangled lives of people Fred Rogers had never met.

Consider the actress Lauren Tewes, best known as the peppy cruise director Julie on the hit ABC series *The Love Boat*, which ran from 1977 to 1986. Tewes left the show in 1984 due to personal problems—mostly, her cocaine addiction. "I thought it gave me the courage I missed," she confessed, explaining the drug's appeal. "It was like going to Oz and asking for courage. But instead, I got cocaine."

Tewes made many bad decisions, as addicts often do, and felt helpless in the face of her own habit. One morning at home, lonely and scared, she heard a familiar sound on her television set: Mister Rogers singing "It's a beautiful day in this neighborhood." He asked television viewers, "Won't you be my neighbor?"—and on that day, Tewes was listening and ready to answer yes. She said, "I realized that in the world, there was someone who really would be my friend." The most straightforward of messages helped Tewes conquer her complicated problems: "I had a glimpse of hope and moved closer from that day to a cocaine-free life."

Fred Rogers was a professional communicator, so for him, depth and simplicity started with his attitude and his words. But he wasn't a man to spout empty platitudes: over and over, his words became deeds. He lived his life the same way he spoke, cutting out the distractions and fripperies so he could focus on what was important. That means his deeds can easily become words again; in this list of ten ways to adopt Mister Rogers' best practices, you will find such fundamental credos as "Be kind to strangers," "Make a joyful noise," and "Share what you've learned." You won't implement these philosophies the same way he did, because you are a different person, but if you follow his example, you will find yourself becoming a better version of yourself, living a life that has more meaning. And the foundation for all of it is "Be deep and simple."

"I feel so strongly that deep and simple is far more essential than deep and complex," Fred told Benjamin Wagner, his young neighbor—his actual neighbor, since the Wagner family rented a house on Nantucket next door to the Rogers family. The phrasing came from the title of a book by Fred's friend Bo Lozoff, *Deep & Simple,* but the values were his own. Wagner was so inspired by this wisdom, and how it helped him reorient his own values, he made a whole documentary (*Mister Rogers & Me*) about it. "Spread the message," Fred told him.

Fred shared the message himself, through the daily example of how he spent his life, through his television programs, and sometimes through more unusual venues. In the 1970s, Hallmark invited Mister Rogers to design a Christmas display for its flagship Manhattan store. Other celebrities also contributed elaborate Christmas set pieces, what one observer called "phantasmagorical decorations." Mister Rogers' offering didn't sparkle or spin or blink. It was a small Norfolk Island pine tree, planted in a transparent box so that its roots would be visible, and completely devoid of any decorations or ornaments. The display had a plaque with a message that was simple but deep: "I like you just the way you are."

Be kind to strangers.

For Patrick Donahue, Fred Rogers wasn't just a beloved figure on the TV screen, but a part of his family's history: Donahue's grandmother had worked for years as young Fred's nanny. So the Donahues got Christmas cards from Mister Rogers every year—and in the spring of 1985, when Donahue was a sophomore at James Madison University majoring in communications, looking for a summer internship, his mother suggested that he write to Mister Rogers.

Donahue sent him a letter, three pages of neat handwriting, along with a picture of his grandmother. About a month later, he got a phone call from Mister Rogers, inviting him to come to Pittsburgh for an interview. After a lunch meeting with everyone's favorite neighbor and David Newell (aka Mr. McFeely), Donahue was offered the internship. When Donahue asked if there were any books he should read to get ready for the job, Mister Rogers recommended *The Magic Years: Understanding and Handling the Problems of Early Childhood,* by Selma Fraiberg, and sent Donahue a copy of his own *Mister Rogers Talks with Parents.*

That summer, Donahue rented a room at a nearby Carnegie Mellon fraternity house for ten weeks and walked to work every day: unlike many TV jobs, this one had steady nine-to-five hours. Donahue helped procure props for the show, driving around Pittsburgh "asking merchants if we could use their wares on *Mister Rogers' Neighborhood*." Before each show was taped, he would bring Mister Rogers his sweater and sneakers, "and on one special occasion, the puppet King Friday." He also appeared briefly on camera—for a scene at Chef Brockett's bakery, local children were serving as extras, but for some reason the parents of two kids had gone missing, so Fred, concerned as always about the children's well-being, asked Donahue to look after them.

Donahue knew he was doing gofer work, but he was happy that he was doing it for a show like the *Neighborhood* that had a positive impact on the world. He learned that "no matter how minuscule your job may be, you can contribute and be part of something that is larger than yourself."

Donahue's memory of the *Neighborhood* set is that it looked much the same in person as it did on TV. "What was unique was that you had a world-class jazz musician in Johnny Costa just off set composing tunes." And "kindness was the culture." At the end of the internship, Mister Rogers unexpectedly wrote a letter to Donahue's parents, telling them how proud he was of Patrick, and of them for being his parents.

Years later, Donahue had given up television for college administration. When he applied for a job at Rollins College, looking to be their director of career services, he didn't tell Fred or Joanne Rogers, even though the Florida school was their alma mater—he didn't want them to pull any strings on his behalf. But soon after Donahue got the job, Mister Rogers walked into his office—he was on his annual vacation at nearby Winter Park—and told him he was taking him to meet the college president, Rita Bornstein. Donahue felt awkward, but Rollins' most famous alum insisted, and they caught Bornstein in the parking lot as she was driving away.

"Rita, please get out of the car," Mister Rogers said. "I want you to meet your new career services director, Patrick Donahue. He is a good friend of mine." After the impromptu meeting, Mister Rogers took a photo of Donahue and Bornstein together.

Back at the career services office, an impressed co-worker told Donahue, "There is no better job security at Rollins College than being friends with Mister Rogers."

Donahue eventually moved on to Indiana University, always carrying the lessons he had learned from Mister Rogers: "Kindness, listening, empathy, and love are eternal gifts from heaven," he said. "And he used those gifts to do more good than any human being I have ever met."

On the wall of Donahue's office at IU, you can find an autographed poster that Mister Rogers gave him on the last day of his internship. The inscription reads, "Patrick, it is good to know you."

Over thirty years later, Patrick Donahue said the feeling was mutual: "It was good for my soul to know Fred Rogers."

BETH USHER WAS IN HER THIRD WEEK OF KINDERGARTEN WHEN SHE fell off the seesaw. That happens to a lot of kids—the unusual part was what came afterward, when Beth started having seizures, as many as a hundred times a day. "It feels like you're on a roller coaster and it keeps going and going and you can't get off," Beth said. She was five years old.

Her only respite was when she watched *Mister Rogers' Neighborhood.* Her mom, Kathy Usher, would prop her up in front of the television and surround her with soft pillows so that Beth wouldn't hurt herself. But it turned out the pillows weren't necessary; during the time the show was on, something about Mister Rogers' voice calmed her brain and her body.

It took the Usher family a couple of painful years before they got an accurate diagnosis—Beth had a rare disease eating away at the left hemisphere of her brain, called Rasmussen's encephalitis—and found a doctor who could fix the problem. That was the brilliant neurosurgeon Ben Carson, later an unsuccessful presidential candidate and the Secretary of Housing and Urban Development in the Trump administration: he would remove the diseased half of her brain. This procedure was legitimately terrifying but had a good chance of success.

The family, nervous about surgery that seemed essential but could kill their daughter, kept canceling and rescheduling the surgery. During this time, Kathy contacted Fred Rogers' offices at WQED and told the person who answered the phone about Beth, hoping that maybe the show could send a signed photo or even an encouraging note that would give her daughter some solace. That night, however, the telephone rang.

Beth said, "My mother spoke to the caller for a few minutes and then told me a friend wanted to talk with me. I was excited that someone calling themselves a friend was calling me. Friendships were difficult. Seizures scared adults—never mind kids. I took the phone from my mother and said hello.

I heard a familiar voice and felt immediately at ease. Mister Rogers asked me about my brain surgery and I told him things that I did not even tell my parents. I told him that I was scared but wanted the seizures to go away. I told him that I wanted the kids in my class to like me and want to play with me. I told him that I was afraid I might die and leave my brother. *Mister Rogers' Neighborhood* characters, King Friday, Lady Elaine Fairchilde, and my favorite, Daniel Striped Tiger, assured me that the doctors and my family would take good care of me. We talked for over an hour. Before I hung up the phone, I said, 'I love you, Mister Rogers.' He told me that he loved me, too."

The family drove from Connecticut to Baltimore for the surgery at Johns Hopkins, listening the whole way to a box of Mister Rogers cassette tapes that he had sent them. Beth's favorite tape was the album where he sang "I Like You Just the Way You Are." As Beth was wheeled into surgery, she told her parents, "No more seizures." The twelve-hour hemispherectomy was a success, but her brain stem swelled more than expected. That night she fell into a coma, which lasted for six weeks.

The Usher family kept a vigil in the intensive care unit, where Beth was plugged into an array of life-support machines. One day, Kathy was called to the nurse's station—there was a phone call from somebody claiming to be Mister Rogers.

Of course, it was the actual Mister Rogers. He had been calling the Usher house every day to check on Beth, and when he didn't hear back, he called the hospital directly. She gave him the unhappy update, and Mister Rogers told her that he would be praying for Beth. (The family had no idea that he was an ordained minister, or that he began every day with a long litany of prayers.)

For two weeks, Mister Rogers checked in every day with the

Ushers—and then he told them that he wanted to visit. Kathy discouraged him, both because he was a busy man and because there were no signs that Beth was about to emerge from her coma. But he insisted—he just wanted a promise that the hospital wouldn't publicize his trip. The next day, he flew from Pittsburgh to Baltimore, carrying only a clarinet case. "It was really amazing because he didn't know us before that," Beth's father, Brian Usher, said.

At the hospital, with family and medical staff peering in from the doorway of Beth's room, Mister Rogers sat with the comatose Beth for an hour. He opened up his clarinet case and pulled out replicas of puppets from the Neighborhood of Make-Believe: King Friday, Lady Elaine Fairchilde, Cornflake S. Pecially, Henrietta Pussycat, and, most important, Daniel Striped Tiger. He sat with Beth, speaking with her gently—and she remained stubbornly unconscious.

After an hour, Mister Rogers had to head back to the airport. He suggested that Kathy take a photo so that when Beth was conscious, she could see that he had visited. Weeks later, Beth finally woke up—and was astonished to find herself surrounded by Neighborhood puppets.

The surgery was a success, meaning that Beth stopped having seizures and was still her lively, intelligent self. But even after she relearned how to walk and talk, she had issues with short-term memory loss, walked with a limp, and lost motor control of her right hand. Mister Rogers remained her friend, calling her on birthdays or when she got a good report card. "Fred didn't always have time, but when there was a child, he made time," David Newell said. "Beth was an exceptional child, so it made perfect sense."

When she was twelve years old, Beth wrote a pamphlet for children entering the hospital, called "The Sun Can Come Out Again, or: How I Got Rid of Something Bad!" She told her story, along with fifty rules of hospital survival (#6: "Pretend you're asleep when people you don't like visit you"). That same year, Mister Rogers gave the commencement speech at the University of Connecticut, where Kathy and Brian both worked, and quoted verbatim Beth's suggestion for what he should say: "I am here to tell you to be friendly to everyone and to do little favors for people. Then they will like you and feel better about the world."

That weekend, Beth finally got to meet her hero in person, while she was awake. "He was just as I imagined he would be," she said. "His voice was so kind and gentle and we gave each other a huge hug. I could not help but cry with sheer happiness and hero worship."

Beth Usher grew up, a commonplace outcome for most children, but something that at one point didn't seem like it was going to happen for her. She never forgot the gift Mister Rogers gave her: he sustained her through the most difficult period of her life. She still treasures the puppets he brought to the hospital because they remind her of their friendship, and she's tried to follow in his footsteps, making the world a better place. "I believe we can heal our world through laughter and good humor," she said. "I love life, my family and friends, and just getting out of bed in the morning. I chose happiness and gratefulness."

SAIHOU OMAR NJIE SPENT HIS CHILDHOOD IN THE GAMBIA, IN western Africa, before coming to the United States in 1985.

He's a fiber artist specializing in batik, an Indonesian process where you apply wax to fabric before dying it: the wax protects the fabric from the dye, so when you finally remove the wax, ghostly patterns remain. (In the Gambia, the principle is the same, but artisans typically use mud instead of wax.)

When Njie made the cover of *Pittsburgh* magazine in 1997—the magazine had an article on local designers—he got a phone call from Fred Rogers, who wanted to talk to him about his art. Njie said, "After a couple of phone calls, he decided he was going to go for it and record an episode. We had several meetings prior to the episode where we discussed a simple way of explaining batik to his young audience." Fred's breakthrough: "Children have candles in their lives on their birthdays—they remember the lighting of the candles." So they used the melting wax from a birthday candle to help small children understand the medium of batik.

"He has a calm demeanor and he's very soft-spoken, but in the studio, he became a different person," Njie said. "Not that he was mean, but he had his idea and he wanted it to turn out like he had thought about it. We spent almost all day doing takes and takes until he was satisfied. He was so set on how the final result would affect his audience. That was his main concern: Would the kids understand it?"

They also decided to showcase Njie's sewing skills, and so he made Mister Rogers a vest out of batik cloth, which the host wore on that episode. Njie likes to brag that he's the one person on the *Neighborhood* who ever got Mister Rogers to wear something other than a cardigan.

Njie's wife and his younger daughter attended the shoot, and he believes that the experience that day pushed his daughter in the direction of being an artist. Njie became a teaching artist, so he now works with young people himself. (Not usually as young as Mister Rogers' audience, admittedly.) "The inspiration came from Fred," he says. "I'm in the classroom most of the time. And whenever I'm teaching, he's always in the back of my mind. Break it down to the simplest element: simplify, simplify."

After they filmed their episode together, Njie and Mister Rogers still saw each other. "One day I was walking down from my studio and he came out of his house," Njie said. "I didn't know he lived right there where my gallery was."

"I saw you walking down the street and thought I'd come out to say hello," Mister Rogers said.

"You could have just opened the window and hollered!"

"An old man needs a walk sometimes."

Since he lived so close to Njie's gallery, Mister Rogers would attend whenever Njie had a new exhibition of his artwork. One time, Njie told him, "Fred, why don't you wait until the end of the day to show up? Because when you show up, you steal my show!" And the two friends laughed together.

Njie said, "I have met a whole lot of people, I have lived around the world, and Fred has been a highlight. I believe that this world is short-lived: we're here for a minute and then we're gone. What we leave behind is what matters. Fred came here on a mission, and when he was all done, he packed up and left. I'm hoping that one day somebody will remember their experience with me and do good work in the world of the future."

MISTER ROGERS HAD DEVOTED VIEWERS HE NEVER COULD HAVE imagined when he started filming the *Neighborhood:* not just children, but adults, people who didn't speak English, and even a western lowland gorilla. That gorilla, named Koko, lived from 1971 to 2018 and achieved great fame for her facility with American Sign Language, which revealed both deeply held emotions and a playful wit. The best Koko story ever is probably the time she ripped the sink out of the wall in her living quarters, and then pointed at her beloved pet kitten, named All Ball, and signed, "cat did it."

The second-best Koko story, however, might be the time Mister Rogers visited her. He flew out to the Santa Cruz mountains in California to Koko's home at the Gorilla Foundation's preserve, looking to film an encounter for a 1998 episode of the *Neighborhood*. He had been warned not to look Koko in the eye. Producer Margy Whitmer accompanied him and was told to wait in a separate area—their visit was expected to be fifteen minutes. Fifteen minutes passed, then twenty, then thirty, and she began to get worried—was her friend and employer getting mauled after accidentally looking the gorilla in the eye? Finally, after an hour, Mister Rogers returned, exhilarated, saying, "That was wonderful!"

Koko, an avid viewer of the show, immediately recognized Mister Rogers as her friend from television. (This is probably the right place to mention that while there was serious academic dispute as to exactly how large Koko's vocabulary was, and some of the claims of her language acquisition were never independently verified, she was also clearly an intelligent gorilla who was a pioneer in cross-species communication.) She took Mister Rogers in her lap, and promptly began a visit with Mister Rogers the way she knew it was supposed to happen: she took off his shoes.

When Koko pulled Mister Rogers onto her lap, he accepted

her embrace, although she weighed twice as much as him and could have seriously injured him if she had wanted to. "He had this innate trust in beings," Whitmer said. He had brought a bag with several gifts for Koko, including a harmonica, a towel decorated with pictures of cats, and a small stuffed Daniel Striped Tiger. Koko rifled through the bag—and then unzipped Mister Rogers' cardigan sweater.

Koko purred with pleasure and blew air softly at Mister Rogers. Her trainer and translator, Penny Patterson, explained that this was a gorilla greeting, and Mister Rogers mimicked her, saying hello back. She smelled his hand, gently touched his face, and then led him by the hand into her bedroom area. There, she removed his sweater, checked his mouth for gold teeth, and initiated a game where he chased her around the bedroom. She played the harmonica for a little while, and then used Mister Rogers' camera to take some pictures. (Koko loved cameras—her first appearance on the cover of *National Geographic*, in 1978, was of her taking a photograph.) She signed a question about his ornate cuff links—were they flowers? The answer was that the cuff links, a gift from his father, were small suns.

"Koko-love," she signed. "Love you visit."

"Well, I love visiting with you," Mister Rogers told her. Before he left, he made the sign for "love."

The only drawback of the visit, according to Whitmer, was that Mister Rogers left reeking of gorilla scent. When they got into their rental car, he was so fragrant that she said, "They are never going to take this car back!"

"HE BLENDED INTO LIFE." THAT'S HOW A SET DECORATOR DESCRIBED Fred Rogers, admiring the way he carried himself without the ego of a star. She knew him because she worked at WQED for most of the 1970s and '80s, back when her name was Cathy Tigano. The WQED studio was also where she fell in love with another co-worker, set carpenter Pat Gianella.

In July 1983, after they had been dating for about a year, Gianella asked Tigano to marry him. She had been married once before; the first time around, she had a full-tilt Catholic wedding, and she wasn't sure she could handle all that hoopla again. So, she joked, she would tie the knot only if "you get Fred to marry us."

Gianella promptly hustled her upstairs to Fred Rogers' office and explained the situation to the only ordained Presbyterian minister on the premises. Much to her surprise, he said, "That would be wonderful! But you'd have to do it this Saturday." After that, he was flying to California to appear on *The Tonight Show* and then going to Nantucket for the rest of the summer.

Their families hustled to make arrangements for a back-yard wedding, and a few days later, Tigano found herself wearing a wedding dress in a bedroom, having a major freak-out, terrified to leave the room.

Somebody knocked on the door: it was the Reverend Fred Rogers, checking on the bride's state of mind. When he saw she was melting down, he soothed her, telling her, "Cathy, there's a lot of love out there. A lot of people would love to see this happen."

She calmed down; Mister Rogers helped comb her hair, and then he helped to blow-dry the groom's hair. "Things are going to be okay for both of you," he told them. "Now let's do this."

She stepped out the back door and was greeted by a sea of flashbulbs, as if she were walking on a red carpet in Hollywood, and not a weather-beaten deck in Pittsburgh. But Mister Rogers' presence was reassuring, and he elegantly offered his blessings on their union—"May they grow in grace and understanding of all that is real and important in life"—and in short order, the happy couple were married.

Before Mister Rogers left, he gave them a stamp of approval that Cathy Tigano Gianella would never forget: "So you met in the Neighborhood of Make-Believe. And now we'll make this real."

ANTHONY BREZNICAN IS A SUCCESSFUL JOURNALIST AND THE AU-thor of the novel *Brutal Youth*, but back in 1996, he was a student at the University of Pittsburgh, and his life wasn't going well. He was lonely, he was unhappy, he didn't know where he was headed. He worked hard at the school newspaper, hoping that writing might be a doorway into a better future but believing that failure was equally possible. And his beloved grandfather had recently died.

But one morning on his way out of his dorm, Breznican passed by a common room where the TV had been left on, tuned to WQED, and Mister Rogers was beginning his show, asking viewers if they would be his neighbor. Nobody was watching—except Breznican. He never sat down, but he watched the whole show, almost hypnotized by the images of the sweater, the trolley, the fish. "His show felt like a cool hand on a hot head," Breznican said.

A few days later, Breznican left the offices of the school newspaper—*The Pitt News*—riding the elevator down to the stu-

dent union. And on the elevator, astonishingly, was Mister Rogers in the flesh: "a slim, old man in a big coat and scarf, eyes twinkling behind his glasses, a small case clasped between his hands in front of him." They nodded at each other, and on the ride down, Breznican desperately tried to stay cool.

Once they stepped out on the ground floor, Breznican waited for a moment and then blurted out, "Mister Rogers . . . I don't mean to bother you. But I just wanted to say thanks."

Mister Rogers smiled at him. He had someplace else he was headed, and he had encounters like this all the time, but at this moment, his full attention was on Breznican. "Did you grow up as one of my television neighbors?" he asked. When Breznican affirmed that he had, Mister Rogers opened his arms wide for a hug. "It's good to see you again, neighbor," he told Breznican.

They walked together, Mister Rogers asking questions of the young man he had just met, wanting to know what he was studying at the university. Breznican told him how much he admired the playing of Johnny Costa. When Mister Rogers opened the door of the student union, Breznican found himself confessing in a tumbling rush of words that recently he had watched the *Neighborhood* for the first time in years, and that it had given him solace at a time when it was much needed.

Mister Rogers listened intently, and then, letting the door shut, stepped back inside. He gestured at a nearby window ledge, where he sat down. Looking into Breznican's eyes, he said, "Do you want to tell me what was upsetting you?"

Breznican sat down next to Mister Rogers, and told him about the death of his grandfather, and the void that his passing had left in his life, and the sorrow that he hadn't been able to share with anybody. In turn, Mister Rogers told him about his own grandfather, the man he had called Ding-Dong, who had always encouraged him and told him how he made every day special. Ding-Dong had died nearly fifty years before, but Mister Rogers still felt his absence, still wished he could talk with him. "You'll never stop missing the people you love," he advised Breznican.

He told Breznican of how one time, his grandfather had bought him a rowboat as a reward for an accomplishment in his life: maybe a good report card, but definitely something he had worked hard to achieve. "He didn't have either now, the grandfather or the boat, but he had that work ethic, that knowledge and perseverance the old man encouraged with his gift."

Mister Rogers advised him, "Those things never go away."

They sat for about five minutes, Mister Rogers passing on what wisdom he could, but more important, showing Breznican that he cared about him—at a moment in Breznican's life when he needed that more than anything. As they parted ways, Breznican thanked him one more time and said that he was sorry if he had made him late for his next appointment.

Mister Rogers smiled at Breznican and told him, "Sometimes you're right where you need to be."

Make a joyful noise.

It's you I like," Rita Moreno sings in a voice sweet enough to serve for dessert. "It's not the things you wear." It's 1975 and Moreno is appearing as a guest on *Mister Rogers' Neighborhood* with her husband and daughter. Standing in his living room with a blue scarf tied loosely around her neck and a crown of curly hair announcing her regal status, she is crooning one of Mister Rogers' signature songs while he accompanies her on piano.

"It's a *pretty* song," Moreno said forty-four years later, still appreciative of Fred Rogers' tunefulness. "His songs were very simple. They were melodic. They're not the kind of thing you'd go on *The Tonight Show* and sing—they weren't meant to be done that way." Moreno knew exactly how the song was supposed to be delivered: plainly and directly at the camera, so that it entered the heart and mind of each child watching the show. At the end of her performance, so nobody could doubt it, she pointed into the camera and told Mister Rogers, "I was singing that to our friend."

Fred Rogers wrote hundreds of songs for his program,

few of them longer than a minute or two. Some of them were used just once, like "Vacuum Sweepers" or "The Neighborhood Burlap Bags." But others topped his personal hit parade, appearing in show after show for decades, until children could not only sing along, but believe in the messages that Mister Rogers expressed through his lyrics.

"Won't You Be My Neighbor?": *Every day, Mister Rogers wants to be your neighbor.* "Many Ways to Say I Love You": *Your parents express their love for you by the way they take care of you.* "I Like to Take My Time": *You don't need to hurry.* "What Do You Do with the Mad That You Feel?": *When you're angry, you can find non-hurtful ways to express your emotions.* "Everybody's Fancy": *Boys and girls have different genitalia, but both genders can take pride in their bodies.* "Let's Think of Something to Do": *Boredom is an opportunity.* "Tree Tree Tree": *Trees are awesome.* "It's Such a Good Feeling": *The world is a wonderful place and I can't wait to share it again with you tomorrow.*

"They were *all* uplifting songs," Moreno said. "What he's saying all the time, in many different ways, is 'You have value. You have worth. The color of your skin is meaningless, in the sense of having value and being a worthy person.' And that is a remarkable thing."

During the seven years of *The Children's Corner,* from 1954 to 1961, when Fred Rogers was producer and puppeteer, he wrote many songs with the show's host, Josie Carey. She wrote the lyrics; he composed the music. "He wrote these beautiful melodies—I thought I'd died and gone to heaven," she said. The collaboration had its frustrations: Carey would spend "hours and hours" on a lyric, and then present it to Fred, who would sit down at the piano and write the music in minutes. Sometimes he would want to write down a melody when he didn't have sheet music around, and so he'd quickly scrawl a musical staff on ordinary paper.

Two of the standout Carey/Rogers compositions were "Goodnight, God," a lullaby that was covered by popular 1950s acts such as Teresa Brewer and the Lennon Sisters, and "Tomorrow," which was the closing song for hundreds of early episodes of *Mister Rogers' Neighborhood*.

Unfortunately, Carey and Rogers foolishly signed away the rights to their songs, enticed by a record company that promised to release their compositions on an album. As a result, Mister Rogers was charged fees to use their old songs on the *Neighborhood* and phased them out in favor of new songs that he wrote without Carey.

Sometimes a conversation with his psychology-professor mentor, Dr. Margaret McFarland, would lead to a homework assignment. "One time we decided that we should write a song about permissible regression," Fred said. (The second "we" in that sentence appears to have been a euphemism for "I.") "Regression in the service of the ego. In other words, slipping back and feeling that it's okay to do younger things in order for you to later go forward." Fred was stymied for quite a while—it was an abstract concept, not one that was easy to reduce into a verse or two that could be understood by preschoolers. But on vacation in Nantucket, sitting in the Crooked House next to the waters of the Atlantic Ocean, he found the words pouring out, verse after verse: "Sometimes you feel like holding your pillow all night long / Sometimes you hold your teddy bear tightly— he's old but he's still strong."

The resulting song, "Please Don't Think It's Funny," is

stately but moving, like a national anthem for a country composed of small children. Mister Rogers performed it thirty-one times on the *Neighborhood,* always making it sound like a friendly conversation. He wouldn't countenance any kind of commercials aimed at children, but he knew the fundamental principle of advertising: repeat impressions were the way to inculcate the message. So he sang the song as many times as he needed to.

The nature of his work was clear, for anyone paying attention. Peggy Charren spent much of her life pushing for higher standards in kids' TV, principally through the advocacy group she founded, Action for Children's Television. She was a perceptive woman with a discerning eye, so when she first saw Mister Rogers in action, she described him thus: "Oh, a singing psychologist for children!"

Consistency was one of the paramount virtues of the *Neighborhood:* Fred made sure that day after day, the show might feature different guests and storylines, but it had the same familiar rhythm. He made an exception, however, for music, specifically the fifteen "operas" he presented on the show where the whole of the program (after Mister Rogers' entrance through the front door) was devoted to a mini-musical drama Fred had written. Strictly speaking, they were better classified as "musicals"—many of them had significant chunks of spoken dialogue—but Fred always called them "operas," a choice that was both grander and funnier. Originally, the operas were commissioned as royal command performances by King Friday XIII, and even credited to the Royal O Room Opera Company (with the admission price sometimes being thirteen hand claps).

Writing the operas, Fred pushed the "whimsy" button as hard as he could, and the results were usually delightful. A show like *Windstorm in Bubbleland* had an environmental moral, but the joy of the show was absurd costuming like François Clemmons dressed up as a porpoise weatherman on *Bubblewitness News,* elaborate sets like the boardroom that looked like the break room on the Death Star, and a great heel turn from Joe Negri, a businessman who melodramatically revealed himself as the evil embodiment of wind sent to blow away all of Bubbleland's bubbles.

Since Fred had cast most of his human ensemble because of their musical ability, the vocal talent was always excellent, with Clemmons being a standout. The emotional heart of the operas was often provided by Betty Aberlin, playing a cat who wishes for a star from the sky but instead learns to twinkle herself; a woman who enters a magical Otherland, rescues her brother, and falls in love with a swan; a cow who wishes she were a potato bug ("Cows don't groove," we learn).

Aberlin took the title role in the fifteenth and final opera on the show, *Josephine the Short-Neck Giraffe.* It was also Fred's first opera: he started writing it as a student at Rollins College, and in 1989, fully thirty-eight years after he graduated, he finally staged it on the *Neighborhood,* filling three episodes. Over the years, he had tinkered with the opera: English lyrics by Josie Carey replaced his original French libretto, he added characters and songs, and he changed the ending. In the final version, Josephine doesn't get the long neck of her dreams, but she learns to be happy with her short-neck self, and to express that joy through song.

Fred Rogers grew up in a house where florid expressions

of emotion were frowned upon, so he learned to be outwardly stoic. But he could use his piano to express his feelings, and he continued that habit as an adult. On the set of *Mister Rogers' Neighborhood,* he wouldn't rant at the production staff if a day's filming was beset with technical difficulties, or if a sequence wasn't coming together as he had expected. Instead, he would sit down at the piano and play—not the chiming melodies he usually favored or the old newsreel tune that he used to signal the end of a shooting day, but loudly, stormily, every brutal note venting his frustrations.

In *Mister Rogers' Neighborhood,* no moment was too small to become musical. "It's a musical grid, this Neighborhood," Fred said. "It's sort of the heartbeat of it all." And because Fred surrounded himself with people who acted like making music was an autonomous body function, he sometimes forgot that not everybody lived in a world suffused with melody, where the most apt metaphor for a developmental challenge was a key change, where music provided the vocabulary to say things that you couldn't express any other way. But sometimes he found out that more people lived in that musical world than he realized.

Visiting New York City on a rainy day, Mister Rogers found himself unable to hail a cab. So, for the first time in years, he descended into the subway system. He found himself on a train filled with schoolchildren—it looked like a class on a field trip. They didn't swarm Mister Rogers but they nevertheless got his attention. "It's a beautiful day in this neighborhood," they sang, softly at first and then louder as one child after another joined the chorus, "Won't you be, won't you be my neighbor?" serenading the man who had helped them grow up.

Tell the truth.

There are tall tales about Fred Rogers. You may have heard some of them yourself: That he was a Navy SEAL in Vietnam who killed dozens of people. That he wore sweaters and long-sleeved shirts to cover up the extensive tattoos on his arms. That he abused children. That he had contempt for his viewers and flipped off the camera.

In the twenty-first century, trying to dispel misinformation and wild celebrity rumors feels a lot like trying to beat back the Atlantic Ocean with a butterfly net. But out of respect for Mister Rogers—and the fundamental concepts of accuracy and reality—let's be as clear as possible: *These stories are not true.* So, what does it mean when so many people believe them and repeat them, either on the Internet or standing in the kitchen of a house party, making conversation while somebody roots around the refrigerator looking for the guacamole? Let's grab our butterfly nets and dive into the ocean.

"Mister Rogers was a U.S. Navy Seal, combat proven in Vietnam with twenty-five confirmed kills to his name. He wore a long-sleeve sweater to cover up the many tattoos on his forearm and biceps. A master in small arms and hand-to-hand combat, able to disarm or kill in a heartbeat. He hid that away and won our hearts with his quiet wit and charm," reads a paragraph that made the rounds of social media in 2003 and beyond. In its favor, it contains English-language words organized in an understandable fashion, but it suffers from being filled with lies from top to bottom.

Mister Rogers, the gentlest of men, never served in the military in any capacity. He never entered basic training or spent time in the ROTC; the institutions he enrolled in were a music conservatory and a seminary. He never killed another human being; in fact, he found most children's cartoons to be excessively violent and steered young relatives away from them. The evidence suggests he never even owned a toy gun as a child. Furthermore, during the years of the Vietnam War, he was busy making television programs in Pittsburgh, so there's ample filmed evidence that he was in a TV studio with puppets on his hands, not in a rice paddy holding a rifle. His longtime floor manager Nick Tallo scoffed at the rumor: "Fred didn't know how to use a screwdriver, let alone kill somebody."

Similarly, his skin was unmarked by any tattoo. He wore sweaters because they ritually signaled the beginning of another television visit. They were also signifiers of adulthood: Mister Rogers was an advocate for children, not a child himself, so he didn't dress like one.

A particularly dark rumor: that as a young man, Mister Rogers abused children and that filming *Mister Rogers' Neighborhood* was his way of doing penance, either on his own initiative or under a court order. Cited as evidence for this lie is the seeming double entendre of the name "Mr. McFeely" and the fact that the show, although aimed at young children, usually has no children appearing on it. This is the rumor that Mister Rogers would have likely found the most appalling and inconceivable, given how it cut against everything he believed and did in life.

And the story that Mister Rogers flipped off the kids watching his show? There is a screen-captured image of Mister Rogers on the set of the *Neighborhood*, with both middle fingers extended—not modified, but deliberately removed from its original context, which is that Mister Rogers was playing a "thumbkins" game where he sang about each finger on the hand in turn.

So why do untrue stories like these take hold in the public imagination? Partially, it's shock value and titillation—people love to be scandalized, love the thrill when somebody is revealed as not being the person they say that they are. Hypocrisy is the easiest sin to condemn in the modern era, since almost everybody has some distance between their public and private selves. You can call a person a hypocrite without, in many cases, even pausing to wonder if you're living up to his or her professed ideals yourself.

It's hard for people to remember that: they've learned so many times that people are not how they present themselves on talk shows or their Instagram feeds, their perpetual question is "No, what's he *really* like?" But although Fred Rogers presented the best version of himself on camera, the public persona of Mister Rogers comported closely to his private self. His wife, Joanne, often said, "With Fred, what you see is what you get." This had the dual advantage of being basically true and waving away attention from the ways in which Fred Rogers was a human being with pride and ego, not a living saint.

On a 1983 trip to New York City, Fred Rogers was standing at the front door to his hotel, waiting for a taxicab—which took some time. Another man, enduring the same wait, said to Mister Rogers, without introduction, "I've never seen you get perturbed before!"

"The funny thing was that I wasn't perturbed at all," Fred commented. "And ten years ago, I'd have worried and worried about what he said—about why someone would want to see me perturbed."

If Mister Rogers was as calm and patient in real life as he was on TV, some people took that not as an inspiration but as an implicit rebuke: Why do *they* get flustered? That's the kind of logic that led a columnist to write in the *Chicago Daily News* in 1968, "Any self-respecting father occasionally wants to punch Fred Rogers right in the nose." The specific argument behind the nose-punching impulse was that it was infuriating to see Mister Rogers get along with children. In a tone that was hyperbolic but appeared to reflect his own conflicted emotions as the father of two young sons, Dean Gysel wrote, "He talks to them as if they were human beings. Something has to be wrong with any man over 30 who likes children."

Since Mister Rogers ended up as a beloved icon with a sweater in the Smithsonian, it can be easy to forget how radical and discomfiting a figure he was when he first appeared on television sets across the nation circa 1968: a plainspoken young man not obviously entertaining his audience, changing out of his work clothes but coming from no specific job, quietly radical in his pacifism, speaking in a "voice that sounds adult to the ears of children and childish to the ears of adults." Adults may not have known what to make of him—hence the nose-punching bluster, hence the lurid rumors—but children knew from the beginning.

Asked why he thought the *Neighborhood* had stayed on the air so long, Fred attributed it to the fact that he was not actually concealing his secret self: "People love honesty," he said. "They like to be in touch with those who are honest and real. Don't you like to be with real people? People who aren't afraid to make mistakes, and people who just know that life is a gift and relish in it?"

Although his show was rigorously scripted, Mister Rogers would sometimes leave in a flub to demonstrate to children that not everything went perfectly for adults. When oceanographer Sylvia Earle came by with a special underwater microphone to use in his fish tank, it broadcast only silence—but Mister Rogers kept the malfunction in the show. When Ella Jenkins led Mister Rogers in a game where he had to touch his body parts in time with a song, he bollixed up the rhythm and was completely out of sync with the song—which he also kept in the show. "He was having fun," Jenkins said with a chuckle. She said that she and Fred were "people who were friends and didn't care if you made a mistake or not."

More fundamental to Mister Rogers' sense of honesty was that he wouldn't deceive children. He hated the idea of getting a child to go to the dentist by saying it was actually a trip to the ice cream parlor. When he did a show about Santa Claus, he successfully walked the tightrope of not lying to kids about the reality of Santa Claus but also not explicitly saying that he was a myth. (Some parents got mad anyway.) Mister Rogers and Chef Brockett each dress up in a Santa Claus costume, but Santa Claus can exist only in the Neighborhood of Make-Believe. There, Santa Claus visits Daniel Tiger, who is worried that Santa is spying on him, since he's heard that he knows when you've been sleeping, knows when you've been awake, and knows if you've been good or bad. Santa assuages Daniel's concerns, telling him "I'm not a spy and I can't see people when they're sleeping."

Speaking with adults, Mister Rogers had all the probity you would expect from a Presbyterian minister: he strove to tell the truth but was sometimes a little loose with the sourcing of anecdotes. If he had a personal fact-checker, she might have flagged how Mister Rogers told a favorite story about a four-year-old boy trusting him enough to confess "I only wear diapers at night now" many times over the years, but the location and time of the meeting changed as necessary. Mister Rogers didn't seek to deceive adults, but some inaccuracies slipped through the cracks. When he was communicating with children, however, he carefully double-checked everything that came out of his mouth to make sure that he wasn't accidentally misleading them.

Fred Rogers' sense of honesty derived from his bedrock principle that everyone was special. "There is only one person in the whole world like you," he said in 1999, and then he nodded sagely, as if he was hearing those words for the first time ever. "That's the greatest gift you can give anybody: the gift of your honest self."

CODA

Journalist Dean Gysel may have had mixed feelings about Fred Rogers, and even thought of punching him in the nose, but he did appreciate how he approached children on their own terms—so when he wrote about him for his newspaper column, he brought along his own five-year-old son, Thane.

"I see you on television," Thane said.

Mister Rogers knelt down so he could look him in the eye, and holding Thane's hand, confided, "I'm a lot bigger here."

Thane then embarked on a monologue about his entire life, from his recent chicken pox to his plans to dig for buried treasure, peppering Mister Rogers with questions: Do you like peanut butter? Do you watch the Three Stooges? Do you know my mother? (Yes; no; no, but I bet you love her very much.)

Afterward, Mister Rogers summarized the conversation: "He wanted to know if we were on the same wavelength. He asked if I liked the same things. It was a test to see if he could trust me." Mister Rogers passed the test; Thane told him that they could ride their two-wheelers together.

Just over one year later, Dean Gysel lost control of his car on a wet road and collided with a tractor-trailer, dying in the crash. As Thane grew up, the memory of his encounter with Mister Rogers faded—but that didn't take away from the day his father brought him to visit with his television friend, who listened carefully to him and answered all his questions honestly.

Connect with other people every way you can.

He honed his craft on local television, starting in the 1950s, gradually developing a repertory company of puppets with distinct personalities, puppets that were both entertainers and expressions of his inner self. He finally broke through to a mass audience in the late 1960s with a hugely successful public-television show that made an indelible impression on multiple generations of children. He was beloved—and lauded as the greatest puppetry talent of his generation.

That's Jim Henson, creator of the Muppets, who went from local coffee commercials to *Sesame Street* and beyond. That description also fits Fred Rogers—except for "the greatest puppetry talent of his generation." Mister Rogers didn't reinvent puppetry or even do anything particularly flashy with it. Many young viewers had no idea that the kind man in the sweater was also doing most of the puppet voices in the Neighborhood of Make-Believe. But he wasn't looking to be celebrated as a master of puppets—he was drawn to the art form because it was one of the most effective ways he found to communicate with children. For Fred Rogers, that was its own reward.

Therese Keane, who once interviewed Mister Rogers for a radio show, remembered that on the day he came to the studio, the radio station's secretary brought her two-year-old daughter to work so she could meet her beloved television neighbor. But when the little girl saw Mister Rogers, she screamed—from her vantage point, he was a terrifying six-foot giant, not the manageable figure she knew from her television screen. Fortunately, Mister Rogers was prepared for situations like this; he always traveled with a case of his puppets. Keane said, "Mister Rogers brought out his television puppets that he carried with him and did a private show for her, taking as much time as necessary to calm her down so she could see Mister Rogers as the figure she knew from television."

Mister Rogers started doing puppet shows to entertain other children in his attic playroom, or to fill time with Josie Carey so there wouldn't be dead air on *The Children's Corner*. But he learned just how intensely children related to puppets, even at his own home. He liked to pull out his puppets and have conversations through them with his own kids. When Fred and Joanne's younger son, John, was just two and a half years old, he was talking with King Friday XIII and told the wee monarch that he wanted to see a movie. The king told him that he would need to ask his daddy about that.

John looked around the room, but couldn't spot his father, so he asked his mother where he was. Joanne told him that he was right next to King Friday. John then zeroed in on Daddy, seeing him as a person again, not just a complicated support system for King Friday, and asked if he could see a movie.

At the Arsenal Family & Children's Center, puppets were Fred Rogers' primary method of interacting with children. He would introduce the puppets carefully in a therapeutic setting, first talking about the puppet, then putting it on his hand and speaking to it, and only then turning the puppet to the child and speaking as it. Sometimes the presence of the puppet was helpful in an obvious way: children would tell Daniel Tiger a secret they might not share with adults, like a six-year-old boy confiding that his sister had locked him in her room. Very young children liked to stick their fingers into the mouths of the puppets, learning that they could trust the puppet not to bite.

Even more interesting was when children took charge of the puppets themselves. They might put a hat on King Friday's head—covering up his crown, the symbol of his authority, thereby removing his power. Fred worked with a thirteen-year-old girl for weeks as she told elaborate ongoing stories with a donkey puppet and a crow puppet, using them as a way to talk about her relationships with her parents and her peers.

Speaking of the children he worked with at the Arsenal center, Fred Rogers said, "I would give them a lot of puppets to play with. Many times, it would help me to know what they were thinking by the choice of the puppet that they made. If they chose the king, well, they might feel authoritarian at that moment and make some pronouncements. If they chose Daniel Tiger, they might be feeling quite shy." That choice was one he could understand, for he made it himself sometimes. "It's a lot easier, even as an adult, for me to have Daniel say, 'I'm really scared. Do you think maybe you could give me a hug?' You know, that would be hard for *me* to say."

Fred carefully studied the work of Madeleine Rambert, a Swiss psychoanalyst who was a pioneer in puppet therapy. He particularly took note of this passage of hers: "Puppetry is a means of valuable transfer which facilitates the expression of the child's unconscious feelings. It is extremely flexible because of its great simplicity and can suit all the child's dreams. It is in some way the material body into which the child projects his spirit. The puppet takes on life when the child takes hold of it. The puppet's being changes each time its manipulation changes."

John Bell, the director of the Ballard Institute and Museum of Puppetry at the University of Connecticut in Storrs, said, "What's notable about Rogers is that he had an obvious and innate belief that puppets could do the job: puppets would be a good way to articulate the ideas that he wanted to convey about how people communicate with each other, what the ideals are of a well-functioning society."

Bell pointed out that hand puppets have a long global history: "They're in China, India, and especially the national hand puppet characters of Europe." England has Punch (and Judy), Germany has Kasperle, Italy has Pulcinella, Russia has Petrushka. "They're the representative character of the nation," Bell said.

Those hand puppets weren't used for therapeutic reasons, but for entertainment and satire. Bell said, "One of the things all these puppet characters do—they are tricksters who speak truth to power. The ability of puppets to get at issues that might be challenging for a human to convey is this really nice ability."

Spencer Lott, who works as a puppeteer on *Sesame Street,* said, "Glove puppets are one of the oldest styles. It does several things well and other things not as well. Because it's a glove, they're great at handling props: you can pick up the baby and throw it out of the stage. They're great for dexterity or any kind of stage combat. I've kind of refallen in love with glove puppets. You can get a lot of acting out of them, you can do a lot of physical bits. Basically, you can do a lot of storytelling with not a lot of puppet, which is exciting."

Mister Rogers provided the movements and voices for a small army of puppets in the Neighborhood of Make-Believe: famous characters such as Daniel Striped Tiger, X the Owl, Henrietta Pussycat, Lady Elaine Fairchilde, King Friday XIII, and Queen Sara Saturday, but also supporting players including Grandpere, Edgar Cooke, Collette, Donkey Hodie, Mrs. Frogg, Tadpole Frogg, Princess Margaret H. Lizard, and Cornflake S. Pecially. ("Many of them were built by Lee Howard," Spencer Lott said. "They were well-made, deceptively complex puppets.") Wearing the traditional black shirt of the puppeteer and sneakers so he wouldn't make extraneous noise, Fred performed with just his voice and the puppets on his wrists. He had a copy of the script pasted in front of him and a TV monitor so he could see how his work looked on camera.

Fred was well aware of the centuries-old traditions of puppetry, and was happy to discard them when necessary, stripping the art form down to basics. Bob Brown, who appeared regularly on *Mister Rogers' Neighborhood* in the 1970s as a marionettist, remembered one conversation he had on camera with Mister Rogers, standing near a pile of twigs they were using for a marionette version of "The Three Little Pigs."

"Your puppets are on strings—how do they work?" Mister Rogers asked.

Brown started to explain, only to be interrupted by Mister Rogers picking up one of the twigs and tying it to a string.

"So, if I tie a string on a twig, I could turn it into a puppet or a marionette?" he asked.

Brown assented, "but in my head I'm going, 'This is the stupidest damn thing. He's dangling this stick on the end of a string and making it dance.' I realized later on, he was really very clever. You couldn't explain how complicated a marionette is and how the strings all work to a two- or a three-year-old, but you tie a single string on a little stick and jiggle it, and the kids get it."

Lott also worked as the puppet captain in *A Beautiful Day in the Neighborhood,* the 2019 movie starring Tom Hanks as Fred Rogers, which meant that he was often re-creating Fred's work. Lott was struck by how little the job had changed since the 1970s. "Being a television puppeteer is still being crammed into a sofa under the castle," he said. "You've got your arms above your head for long takes—take after take after take—you're watching your performance on a monitor, you're picking up props, you're hitting your cues, you're trying to find your light. All the things we do in 2019, it's all the same. He was stuffed in that castle for so many hours and I know exactly what that feels like."

To replicate Fred Rogers' puppetry style, Lott had to get inside his head, which turned out to be a pretty good place to spend some time. "I have grown to love his puppetry. I find it so telling that his puppetry style reflects his mission and its stillness," Lott said. "With his puppetry, less is more, just like his show and his writings. For example, if his puppets move, they're punctuating an idea or a thought. So, the puppets do larger, more theatrical gestures, but in between thoughts, his puppets go back to 'puppet neutral,' so you can move on the action. And there's lots of listening, which he was a big fan of."

Lott noted that puppetry experts would likely critique Fred's lip-syncing abilities. "Most of his characters don't have moving mouths—but even the puppets that do have moving mouths, the show is not known for its lip-sync," Lott observed. "On *Sesame Street*, every Muppeteer, we train so hard to get a mouth flap for every syllable, even though most Muppeteers would agree that what's important is whether the character is connecting with the audience. Fred's lip-sync is all over the place, but if you're able to get past that, there's some gems. King Friday will often travel into a scene by climbing this invisible staircase—a traditional theatrical device, and such a fun little quirk. Sometimes you see the puppets travel, and Lady Aberlin will be wearing the puppet and holding it at the feet, as if she's carrying him. The way that Daniel is built—just fabric and fur—it's super-soft and super-malleable, and it needs to be protected."

Mister Rogers acknowledged that his puppetry wasn't flashy. "I don't know that it was intentionally amateurish at the beginning," he confessed. He had been working to the best of his abilities, but his lack of polish had unexpected benefits. "If they asked me to do slick stuff now, I wouldn't do it," he said in 1983. "One reason we do what we do is to encourage children to believe they can make their own puppets when the show is off the air."

Bell said, "Puppeteers often get into that field because they're not actors. Puppeteers are a bit shy and unforthcoming, and some of that is reflected in Rogers' demeanor as a performer." But even after Mister Rogers started appearing on camera, his show had access to a magical kingdom where the usual rules of storytelling and physics didn't have to apply. "That's a really great possibility for puppetry," Bell said.

Lott concluded, "Spending time in that world, I was inspired by his mission. He was a showrunner to be reckoned with—he had to stick to his morals and he made very specific artistic choices. Now when a job offer comes in, I can look at my wife and say, 'Am I using my tools and my skills for good? Is it passing the Fred test?'"

Love your neighbors.

Fred Rogers, Andy Warhol, George Romero. Three of the great creative minds of the twentieth century, with artistic concerns so different—songs/paintings/movies about kindness/celebrity/zombies—that it's a fun party game to imagine the mash-ups when two of them trade places. (*Fred Rogers' Interview* magazine, where the proprietor regularly reminds interview subjects that he's grateful they were born! Silkscreen portraits of Henrietta Pussycat and Lady Elaine Fairchilde! *Mister Romero's Neighborhood*, where the host barricades the front door to keep out zombie versions of Chef Brockett and Mr. McFeely!)

Although these three geniuses each spent most of their lives in a combination of

Pittsburgh and New York City, and their careers intersected in surprising ways, they mapped out three very different territories on our cultural map. But they had something in common: to create their work, all three needed to create artistic communities of kindred spirits.

Andy Warhol, like Fred Rogers, was born in 1928 in western Pennsylvania. While Fred was the eldest (and for a long time, only) child of one of the most prosperous families in Latrobe, Andy was the fourth child of the working-class Warhola family, immigrants from Austria-Hungary, in Pittsburgh. Andy, like Fred, was afflicted with childhood health problems—most notably Saint Vitus' dance (the colloquial name for Sydenham's chorea), which gave him shaky limbs and a splotchy complexion.

Both the Rogerses and the Warholas doted on their sickly children, buying everything each family could afford: air conditioners and puppets and musical instruments for Fred, comic books and Hershey bars and cutout books of dolls for Andy. Both children were constantly teased and bullied at school, but each one used his artistic bent to entertain other children one-on-one in the family's attic: Fred put on puppet shows for them, while Andy drew their portraits.

As adults, Andy and Fred had lives that ran on parallel tracks in many ways: they were both regular churchgoers, both known for trademark fashion accessories, both shy but deeply curious about other people, both leaders of a cadre of artists who followed them for decades. As Rob Sheffield wrote for *Rolling Stone,* "The two have a strange spiritual kinship, from their speaking voices—that slow-motion 'oh gee' tone—to the way they surround themselves with a factory of damaged, vulnerable creatures who need constant attention." Those uncanny similarities bring their extremely different personalities into higher contrast.

Andy and Fred were both raised as faithful Christians: Andy a Catholic, Fred a Presbyterian. Fred Rogers, ordained as a minister, was obviously more devout. He looked forward to church services, even arranging his travel schedule so he could be home in Pittsburgh on Sundays, worshipping at the Sixth Presbyterian Church. He wanted to understand the mysteries of God's love as profoundly as he could.

Andy Warhol also went to church every Sunday. When he was in the hospital in 1968, fighting for his life after being shot by the disgruntled author Valerie Solanas—he endured five hours of surgery and at one point was declared clinically dead—he promised God that if he lived, he would go to church every Sunday. He skipped confession (he was worried priests would recognize him and gossip about his sins), which meant he had to eschew Communion, and he didn't like to sit through Mass, but he would dart into church between services, find an empty pew, and quickly pray, legalistically fulfilling his pledge to God.

Warhol had no interest in going deeper into what Catholicism offered—but there was nobody in the world better at considering the surface of things. The hours he spent in church as a child, staring at the gilded saints, informed how he presented celebrities like Marilyn Monroe and Elvis Presley, making them into modern golden icons. And his fascination with the exterior life gradually led him to a richer interior life, if not one he publicized: he attended church more frequently as the years went by and even volunteered at the Church of the Heavenly Rest, distributing food to the hungry.

Fred and Andy both had a uniform they donned for their public personas. Mister Rogers was famous for changing into sneakers and a cardigan sweater, a comforting ritual at the beginning of every episode of *Mister Rogers' Neighborhood*. When Andy Warhol got his first big paycheck—an advertising commission for a series of fashion illustrations in the *New York Times*—he spent the money on "one hundred identical white shirts from Brooks Brothers." But he decided that wasn't enough of a trademark look: one day in the mid-1960s, he started wearing a silver-white wig, so ludicrously fake that people assumed it had to be his real hair, because why would anyone wear a wig that obvious? He carried it off through force of will and the power of repetition: by the time he died, anyone putting on a silver wig was self-consciously trying to look like Andy Warhol, the same way he had always tried to look like Andy Warhol, before he even knew what that meant. Similarly, you can't dress up as Mister Rogers for Halloween unless you wear a cardigan sweater.

Both Fred and Andy were shy and preferred to hear about other people rather than talk about themselves. Fred was a famously difficult interview for journalists, not because he was hostile, or even vaguely unfriendly, but because he would curiously ask questions of whoever was talking to him. This was equal parts an effort to get to know them (and maybe to minister to them) and to deflect the conversation away from himself. Reporters who weren't careful would end up with an audiocassette full of them sharing all their problems with Fred Rogers, one of the world's great listeners.

Andy Warhol had a different array of techniques for swatting away press inquiries: he sometimes would lie (announcing at a museum opening that he had become too famous, so he was legally changing his name to John Doe) or offer an over-the-top statement like "Art is what you can get away with," remaining totally deadpan, and waiting for someone to respond.

Warhol loved hearing about other people's lives: he required a constant flow of confessional conversation from his assistants, and would call his employees after hours, speaking only enough to get them talking. He wanted gossip: ideally celebrity dish, but failing that, gossip about their own lives, about art-world figures they knew, about their relatives in the suburbs whom he would never meet. Warhol wasn't asking questions because he hoped for a deeper understanding of his employees' hopes and dreams, which he could then nurture, like Fred Rogers, or even to collect an index of dirt that could provide later leverage—he was asking questions because he found the world to be a scary place and so he lived vicariously through people. Behind his poker face, he reveled in every spat, every petty vendetta, every broken heart.

Both Andy Warhol and Fred Rogers leveraged their success with a core product—children's TV shows, paintings—to release an array of brand extensions. Mister Rogers was lauded for not marketing *Neighborhood* toys to children, but there were still books—more than thirty of them, from *Going on an Airplane* to *Many Ways to Say I Love You*—and record albums and videos. Similarly, Andy Warhol parlayed his art-world success into a magazine (*Andy Warhol's Interview*), a rock band (the Velvet Underground), a series of multimedia happenings (the Exploding Plastic Inevitable), and over one hundred movies, some experimental, some narrative, many in a blurry area in between.

Warhol's headquarters for all this productivity was the Factory—for many years, a studio covered with silver paint and aluminum foil. To produce silkscreens, lithographs, and movies with maximum efficiency, Warhol surrounded himself with assistants and the actors he called Superstars: heiresses, transvestites, and a host of damaged, beautiful people, clamoring for the attention of the public and their silver-wigged patron.

Fred Rogers had staffers who worked on books and other projects, and he had a repertory company of his own. According to Betty Aberlin, the most prominent member of that ensemble, "The earliest days were the best because nobody had become the icon yet. Just a great deal of devotion." She said they were "mostly trying to let people know what we ourselves, many of us, didn't know: that we had worth as is."

A group of performers can sometimes feel like the Island of Misfit Toys: damaged people seeking approval to fill their various emotional voids. The Superstars had to learn that adoration was fleeting, both from the public and from Warhol. The cast of the *Neighborhood* not only found that they had become iconic as Mister Rogers' neighbors—many of them felt personally enriched by the time they had spent in his presence. Aberlin said, "I think we all stayed. We either died or stayed until the end."

Fred Rogers, growing up rich, had a blithe indifference to

money; Andy Warhol, having worked his way through school washing dishes and peddling vegetables from a cart, spent his life obsessed with it. Andy and Fred moved to New York City within a couple of years of each other (1949 for Andy, 1951 for Fred). After two years, Fred was eager to return to Pennsylvania and live in Pittsburgh. Andy, on the other hand, never looked back after he left Pittsburgh: the life he wanted, filled with glamour, glory, and greenbacks, was all in Manhattan. He even brought his mother to live with him in New York City, but he did still have family in Pittsburgh: one of his cousins, Ted Warhola, was the first floor manager of *Mister Rogers' Neighborhood*.

"He didn't want to talk about his cousin," remembers *Neighborhood* crew member Nick Tallo, who worked as the assistant floor manager under Warhola before assuming his job. "In 1969, he probably thought his cousin was batshit."

Sometimes Andy and Fred could sound eerily alike. "Everybody should like everybody," Andy Warhol once said, which is not very far off from Mister Rogers telling millions of viewers, "I like you just the way you are." Andy's statement became a Pop Art manifesto, alongside his beliefs that "everybody should be a machine" and "A Coke is a Coke and no amount of money can get you a better Coke than the one the bum on the corner is drinking."

Pop Art relied on a flattened hierarchy: not only were Brillo boxes and Campbell's soup cans suitable subjects for paintings, but people could consume the artwork as automatically as they might swig one bottle of Coke after another. The mechanical consumption of art was like the mechanical production of art, and the art gallery where artists and collectors met was just like a supermarket, only with fewer items for sale. Growing up in a steel-forging city like Pittsburgh encourages both indefatigability—living in the provinces, you know you will have to work twice as hard if you want to break through in New York City—and a tendency to think of artistic production in industrial terms.

Just as artists often spend their days doing the same thing over and over, making one more variation on a theme that has become their style, television production can be a tedious exercise in retakes and repetition. But when Mister Rogers told his viewers that he liked them just the way they were, he wasn't trying to turn them into an indistinct, lovable crowd: he was celebrating that each one was special, and that consequently, his relationship with each one was unique. Andy Warhol glorified how modern mass culture provided democratic, identical experiences for millions of people; Fred Rogers celebrated the ability to transcend that.

George Romero, born in 1940, was a bit younger than Warhol and Fred Rogers. Romero directed nineteen movies, including *Night of the Living Dead* and its five sequels, which basically created the genre of zombie movies. Romero also worked on the Pittsburgh/New York City axis but had the reverse trajectory of Andy Warhol: he grew up in the Bronx, went to college in Pittsburgh (the Carnegie Institute of Technology, now Carnegie Mellon University), and stayed in town after he graduated.

Night of the Living Dead, his 1968 feature-film debut, was a lean, gripping movie filmed in black-and-white that felt like a social-drama documentary as much as a horror film. Vincent Canby, reviewing it for the *New York Times*, was famously dismissive, describing it as "a grainy little movie acted by what appears to be nonprofessional actors" and "made by some people in Pittsburgh."

In the 1960s, anybody who wanted to make movies or TV shows in Pittsburgh had to build their own infrastructure. Pittsburgh had five TV stations and three film processing labs, but not much else in the way of production facilities. When Romero got out of college, he and a few friends had access to a Bolex motion-picture camera and some cheap lights, which was enough to start a company called The Latent Image and to advertise themselves as "Producers of Industrial Films and Television Commercials."

"We got jobs," Romero marveled. "People actually hired us to make industrial films and television commercials for them."

Some of Romero's earliest jobs were short films commissioned by *Mister Rogers' Neighborhood* and shown on Picture-Picture: "Things with Wheels," "Things That Feel Soft," and "How Light Bulbs Are Manufactured." For that one, crew member Nick Tallo traveled with Romero to a lightbulb factory in New Jersey. Comparing Fred Rogers and George Romero, Tallo said, "Totally different genres—puppets and zombies—but both of the men behind all that were really warm, wonderful guys."

The Picture-Picture film that Romero remembered best was the mini-documentary "Mister Rogers Gets a Tonsillectomy." (It also marked a rare appearance on *Mister Rogers' Neighborhood* by Fred's wife, Joanne Rogers—she accompanied him to the hospital for his surgery.) Romero said, "It was shot in a real, working hospital. I had to quickly, and quietly, use my pin-lights to get exposure in the waiting room, in Fred's bedroom, and in the OR. I still joke that 'Mister Rogers Gets a Tonsillectomy' is the scariest film I've ever made. What I really mean is that I was scared shitless while I was trying to pull it off."

Armed with his *Neighborhood* experience, Romero scrounged together money, equipment, and cash, and made *Night of the Living Dead* for just $114,000, helped by volunteers agreeing to play extras and showing up with free entrails from the butcher shop. For the starring female role of Barbara, who gradually descends into madness, Romero wanted to cast local actress Betty Aberlin, but Fred Rogers wouldn't allow his leading lady to take the role.

Once *Night of the Living Dead* was completed, Fred was, unexpectedly, a big fan. "He loved the film," George said. "He came and loved it. He was always a huge supporter over the years." (Fred enjoyed works of art beyond the parameters of the *Neighborhood*. He once attended a student production of the scabrous Edward Albee play *Who's Afraid of Virginia Woolf?*—distracting cast members who found it hard to spit out the venomous dialogue with Mister Rogers kindly gazing at them from the middle of the front row. After the show, he visited backstage and joked with the actors, "I'm sure glad you don't live in my neighborhood!")

Tallo stayed friendly with Romero and worked on many of his movies, even getting an acting role in 1978's *Dawn of the Dead* as a motorcycle raider. "In the daytime, I'd be in the Neighborhood of Make-Believe," Tallo said. "I'd come home, take a shower, and go to the mall and kill zombies all night. I'd come home and I'd have blood on me, so I'd have to take another shower before I went back to the Neighborhood of Make-Believe."

George Romero wanted to make movies that didn't star the undead—his favorite film was the 1951 operatic fantasy *The Tales of Hoffmann* and his first film after *Night of the Living Dead* was a romantic comedy called *There's Always Vanilla*. But he soon found out that what the world really wanted from him was one zombie movie after another. George approached the artistic assembly line with less enthusiasm than Andy or Fred, but he too had a crew of loyalists who made it possible.

Romero eventually decamped for Toronto—like Fred Rogers decades before him, he found that it was the only place he could realize his vision on film. The central metaphor of Andy Warhol's work was the assembly line, churning out a supply of art as reliably as Ford made Thunderbirds or MGM made musicals. But the central metaphor of George Romero's work was an army of zombies, unrelenting creatures, fueled by hungers they can't explain, coming incessantly until they got what they needed. From Romero's perspective, modern society defined citizens primarily as consumers: of clothes, of Thunderbirds, of movies.

As everyone making movies at the Factory learned, a central metaphor can define the behavior of the viewers and the people behind the camera. To make a movie, especially outside Hollywood, you need to overcome a hundred daily obstacles, always moving forward as insatiably as the walking dead. That relentless hunger can wear anybody down—but Romero got to purge his frustrations by collecting a cadre of loyalists and making classic movies that showed the terrible, bloody results that come when society falls apart.

With his own assortment of loved collaborators, Fred Rogers made himself responsible for the other side of the equation. Day after day, he reminded us of the work that's required for neighbors to come together, and showed people that it was time well spent: in sweet times and sour times, we all need a community.

Find the light in the darkness.

On a high shelf in Tony Cartledge's office, he keeps pictures of a man in a red sweater and a little girl in a flower-print dress. You know the man's name; the girl is called Bethany. They are bound together in a story of grief and solace and inspiration.

Tony leans back in his chair and, fortified by nothing stronger than a diet soda—he is a divinity-school professor, after all—he smiles thinly and remembers the worst day of his life, January 18, 1994. Tony was the pastor at the Woodhaven Baptist Church in Apex, North Carolina, where his wife, Jan, was the minister of education and youth. Their daughter, Bethany, was seven years old: giggly, spunky, famous with her second-grade classmates for always telling jokes. She had just spent a week of her Christmas break visiting with Tony's parents in Lincolnton, Georgia, exploring, playing dress-up, and sleeping in her father's childhood bedroom.

Tony had spent that week leading a ski trip for the youth group at his church. He drove down to Georgia to pick up Bethany; after breakfast, Bethany brushed her teeth without being asked and changed into a white turtleneck and the purple tracksuit she had gotten for Christmas. While Tony loaded up his 1986 Oldsmobile Cutlass, Bethany chatted on the phone with her mother in North Carolina, letting her know that she'd be seeing her soon.

Four hours later, they were on Highway 1, in the middle of South Carolina. Bethany had told her father all the highlights of her week and as many knock-knock jokes as she could remember. Around 11:30 A.M., as they drove through the tiny town of Middendorf, Bethany said she'd like to stop at the next Hardee's so she could have fried chicken for lunch. Tony agreed—and then realized that a black pickup truck driving the other way had drifted across the double yellow lines into their lane. With the vehicles closing at high speed, Tony veered left—and narrowly avoided disaster. But only for a split second.

The pickup truck went off the road and onto the shoulder, which jarred its driver out of his drunken stupor. The driver jerked the car back onto the road—T-boning Tony's Oldsmobile, ripping off its front passenger door, and spinning the car into a ditch.

Tony blacked out. When he came to, the car was surrounded by police and EMTs and a freelance photographer. "I was broken up pretty badly," Tony says. "I had a bit of a concussion, I had seven broken ribs and a punctured lung and my right arm was pretty much in shambles. I wasn't bleeding except from where the windshield glass peppered my face."

Once he regained consciousness, he frantically checked on Bethany. She was right next to him, motionless. The tip of her tongue was sticking out of her mouth, and it had turned blue. Bethany had died immediately, her skull caved in by the impact with the pickup truck. Tony went to the hospital; his daughter went to the morgue.

Tony spent a couple of weeks in the hospital, undergoing various surgeries; during this time, he missed Bethany's funeral. When he finally emerged, his body was patched up but his spirit was shattered. He went home, feeling completely incapable of resuming his ministerial work: How was he supposed to make sense of this senseless tragedy, let alone get into the pulpit and make his grief instructional for his congregation?

The one thing he knew was that he didn't want anyone to tell him that it was God's will, or that everything happened for a reason, or that Bethany had died because God needed another rose in his garden. "It's a cop-out," Tony says, shaking his head. "It makes 'em feel better if they can say it's God's will because then it takes it out of their hands."

With his right arm in a sling, Tony wasn't sleeping much, but he could stay up and write. A member of his church who worked for IBM arranged for the loan of a laptop (a newish technology in 1994), so Tony could sit in an armchair and type with his left hand. He wrote poetry about Bethany, listing some of her favorite earthly things, like saddles and fish sticks. And he wrote letters to people who had played significant roles in Bethany's life, thanking them for the love and care they had shown her. Most of those letters were to friends and family, but one of them went to Fred Rogers; Tony and Bethany had watched *Mister Rogers' Neighborhood* together, weekday afternoons at five o'clock.

"From the time she was two years old," Tony laboriously typed, "Bethany and I made it a habit to watch *Mister Rogers'*

Neighborhood together whenever we could. We sang with you, and fed our fish, and learned about so many things from the films that Mr. McFeely brings. We played in the land of make-believe, and met many wonderful friends. Most of all, we knew—Bethany knew—that she was special, just by being herself. Bethany was in love with life and in love with herself, and while I know that self-esteem derives from many sources, I am convinced that your daily reassurance that she was 'special' had something to do with the quality of her life."

Tony thought that he might, in due time, receive a form letter in return, but a week later, the phone rang. Jan answered the phone and when she heard the gentle voice of Fred Rogers, she soon found herself sobbing. After a tearful conversation, she handed the phone to Tony. "Mister Rogers was just so pastoral, so kind," Tony marvels. "He wanted to hear about what happened and to thank me for the letter. He assured us that he would be praying for us—he had this long list of people he prayed for every day—and asked me to pray for him."

Tony removes his glasses and dabs his eyes, remembering anew how much he needed that call from Mister Rogers. (He encouraged Tony to call him Fred, but Tony still finds it difficult to call him anything other than "Mister Rogers" when speaking with other people.) Before they hung up, Mister Rogers encouraged him to stay in touch.

And Tony did, sending him letters and poems and newsletter articles, and receiving in return letters and cards, written with a teal Flair pen. Over and over, Mister Rogers told Tony what a special person he was and how much he valued his friendship.

Tony told Mister Rogers about a shooting star Jan had seen,

and how they saw it as a message from Bethany, a divine symbol of hope and reassurance. When Mister Rogers sent the
bereaved parents a copy of his book *You Are Special,* he under-
lined the "Are" in the title and added below his inscription,
"May you see all manner of 'shooting stars' all life long."

For a time, Tony and Jan were involved with Mothers
Against Drunk Driving. (The man who killed Bethany had
worked an overnight shift at a ball-bearing factory before pa-
tronizing a nearby bar where he started drinking Bud Ice at
7 A.M., leaving four hours later with a staggering blood alcohol
level of .203.) When they told Mister Rogers that they would
be attending a national MADD meeting in Pittsburgh, he encouraged them to visit his office at WQED.

At the station, they weren't escorted back from the receptionist's desk by a flunky: to their surprise, Fred Rogers
emerged to greet his friends. He was wearing a turtleneck shirt
underneath a blazer, Tony remembers with a chuckle: "I was
so disappointed he didn't have his sweater on." Mister Rogers hugged his visitors. "My first impression was how small he
was," Tony says. "But he could give a big hug." He shakes his
head, still marveling. "It's just amazing to be hugged by Mister
Rogers."

Tony and Jan spent an hour in his office. It was a snug room
with two shabby couches and walls filled with art and plaques.
Tony could read Greek and Hebrew because of his seminary
training, but he told Mister Rogers that he couldn't read the
scroll that had Chinese calligraphy on it.

"Well, I can't read it, either," Mister Rogers said, "but they
told me it means 'If you want to see yourself clearly, don't look
in muddy water.'"

"I *loved* that," Tony says. "I've quoted that so many times. I have often said that Mister Rogers was a clear pool in which people could see themselves as they were, not muddied up by all the people who say you're not good enough or there's something wrong with you. He would reflect back their true value."

Mister Rogers patiently answered Tony and Jan's questions, telling them about his life and work, but he was obviously more interested in hearing about them and their travails. When it was time for them to go, he gave them a pack of a hundred postcards as a memento, each one with a picture of Mister Rogers surrounded by his puppets. The flipside bore the message "MISTER ROGERS' NEIGHBORHOOD is a place where neighbors help each other find within themselves the courage to grow." Mister Rogers took a picture of Tony and Jan, and then got David Newell (in the office that day in his capacity as PR rep for the show, not as Mr. McFeely) to photograph the three of them together.

Tony stayed in touch with Mister Rogers over the years, although he tried not to impose unduly on his time—he knew other people needed the man's care and love, including Fred Rogers himself. He saw him just one other time, when Mister Rogers spoke to the graduating class of North Carolina State in Raleigh: he invited Tony and Jan to be his guests, so they sat in the university president's box and watched Mister Rogers inspire thousands of young men and women as they started their adult lives. In return, the graduates honored him by singing "Won't You Be My Neighbor?" to him.

Afterward, there was a luncheon in the field house at Carter-Finley Stadium, with forty or fifty guests. Mister Rogers sat at the head table—but before he could eat a bite, he spotted a young boy just outside the dining room, standing at the glass door and looking in. Tony said, "He got up, left his lunch, left all the bigwigs at the head table, and he walked around and opened the door and invited the little boy to come in. The boy's father was there—he had brought him on a motorcycle. He'd heard that Mister Rogers was going to be there. He did not look like the kind of guy who would bring his kid to see Mister Rogers, but there he was."

Many years after Bethany died, Tony and Jan split up; once again, he found that life went on. Looking back now, he strongly resists any suggestion that Bethany died so that he could meet Mister Rogers, or for any other divine purpose— but he believes that even after a tragedy, you need to be open to the possibility of good things happening. Mister Rogers granting his friendship and ministering to Tony was precious. Then Tony had to make sense of what the gift meant to him and be a good steward of it. "He was just the most generous, forgiving, accepting person," Tony says. He knew that he couldn't live up to Mister Rogers' standard—but he also knew that the effort was worth making.

"It was instrumental to my recovery knowing that Mister Rogers was praying for me and he cared about me," Tony says. "But more than anything, it impressed on me how much I wanted to be more like him. It's easy to be judgmental; it's easy to be self-centered." So, after Mister Rogers died in 2003, Tony did what he could to carry on his legacy.

As a professor at Campbell University in North Carolina, Tony no longer delivers regular sermons; instead, he teaches classes on writing and the Old Testament. But on a recent Thanksgiving, he was invited to be the chapel speaker at Campbell, and he went full Fred. Tony hid in a storeroom at the back of the chapel until it was time to begin the sermon—at which point a pianist started playing "Won't You Be My Neighbor?" Tony came out singing "It's a beautiful day in this neighborhood," changing from his jacket into a zip-up red sweater and slipping on some blue tennis shoes, bought for the occasion.

Knowing that he wasn't Mister Rogers, Tony tried to pass on his philosophy anyway. *Love yourself. Love your neighbor as yourself. Be thankful.* At the end of the sermon, Tony told the congregants about the pack of a hundred postcards that Mister Rogers had given him many years before. He still had seventy-five of them, he said, and if anyone wanted one—"To use as a bookmark or stick on your mirror as a reminder of how one person embodied Jesus' love, you're welcome to come and pick one up." Dozens of people lined up, eager to receive a card.

Tony's office has mementos from different parts of his life: shards of pottery from an archaeological dig in the Holy Land, original *Kudzu* art commemorating the years he spent working at the Baptist State Convention of North Carolina. But on that high shelf, a teddy bear and a Daniel Striped Tiger puppet are inches away from each other. The symbols of Bethany and Mister Rogers are adjacent on that shelf, just as they are in Tony's memory. "He brought hope to me at that point in life," Tony says simply. "His faith was very deep and very certain. I appreciate that about him, and I wish I was as confident as he was. But the older I get, the less I know, and in some cases the less I believe—so I cling to hope."

Always see the very best in other people.

For a television superstar, Fred Rogers watched remarkably little TV. He was pranked on a 1998 episode of *Candid Camera:* at a hotel filled with network executives and critics attending an annual TV conference, host Peter Funt had set up one room so there was no working TV set (but there was a hidden camera). Mister Rogers checked into the hotel and was duly shown the gimmicked room—but foiled the premise of the bit by completely failing to be frustrated or flustered by the absence of a TV set. That was partially because he was one of the most even-tempered people in the USA, and partially because he genuinely didn't care: if there had been a television, he wouldn't have turned it on.

"You are the first person who's said, 'I don't even need a TV,'" Funt (disguised as a bellhop) told him.

"I have enough TV in my life," Mister Rogers explained.

Usually, Fred Rogers had, at most, one other show that he liked to watch. Through the 1970s, it was the wholesome family drama of *The Waltons*, about a large family living in rural Virginia in the 1930s. In the 1990s, he found another series about a good-hearted family in simpler times: *Dr. Quinn, Medicine Woman*, set in the frontier town of Colorado Springs shortly after the Civil War. Fred befriended the creator of *Dr. Quinn*, Beth Sullivan, and even made a cameo appearance in the show's fourth season, as the Reverend Thomas, mentor to the town's preacher—demonstrating that while he was always a reassuring on-screen presence, he didn't have much acting talent per se, and that it was weird to see him on TV wearing something other than a cardigan sweater.

Fred became a huge fan of *Monty Python's Flying Circus* when it started airing on American television in 1974, bringing home videocassettes of episodes to share with his family. The show was ruder and crasser than his own work—if pie-throwing was an abomination, then what to make of a dance where grown men slap each other with fishes?—but he responded to its whimsy, its surreal humor, and the undeniable genius of the "dead parrot" sketch.

In modern culture, we tend to reduce complicated people to just one or two attributes: that rapper is unhinged, that politician is insincere, that guitarist is a cad. Fred Rogers, while a complex human being in his personal life, spent his life trying to be the public representation of kindness and concern for children. That was admirable, since the world is a better place with an avatar of those values walking among us—but it left him especially vulnerable to being caricatured in other forms of popular culture.

Sometimes, other television programs would refer to Mister Rogers without reducing him to a single dimension. Before Tom Hanks portrayed Fred Rogers in *It's a Beautiful Day in the Neigh-*

borhood, his son Colin Hanks played the man in an episode of *Drunk History,* where the show rambled through the Mister Rogers biography in its trademark unhinged-but-affectionate style. And surprisingly, the hit 1980s sitcom *Family Ties* had a nonobvious joke about the *Neighborhood,* perhaps because the dad, played by Michael Gross, worked at an Ohio public-television station. A colleague complained about Fred Rogers' work habits, asking "Why can't he change his shoes *before* the show?"

Sometimes Mister Rogers was evoked as an impossible ideal, one that people can mimic but not live up to. Pop-punk band Ugly Kid Joe had a 1992 MTV hit with "Neighbor," which borrowed the line "Won't you be my neighbor?" for its chorus, just to underscore how unpalatable it would be to live next door to the group. In Weezer's 2019 music video for their song "High as a Kite," the band plays in "Mister Rivers' Neighborhood," and lead singer Rivers Cuomo walks into a close copy of the familiar living room, starting by changing into sneakers and donning a cardigan (even doing Mister Rogers' move of zipping it up all the way and then down just a bit). But just as the song's lyrics turn from the wholesome high of parasailing to an unsettling effort to escape earthly existence, the video shows how Cuomo can't live up to the idyllic setting of the *Neighborhood,* even backed up by a drummer in a chef's hat. As the lights strobe and Cuomo trashes the set, the children in the studio audience first look bored and then start to cry.

More often, Fred Rogers is evoked so everyone can have a good laugh at him acting out of character. A classic bit on the Canadian sketch-comedy show *SCTV* was "Battle of the PBS Stars," where Rogers (played by Martin Short) dukes it out in the boxing ring with Julia Child (Catherine O'Hara), ultimately winning dirty when he whacks her repeatedly on the head with a King Friday puppet. "I certainly hope the young fans of *Mister Rogers' Neighborhood* aren't staying up to watch this bloody travesty," says announcer Howard Cosell (Eugene Levy). "I don't have to explain. You saw it. He beat the woman unconscious with a puppet."

When Bart and Milhouse temporarily run the Android's Dungeon comic-book store in the 2001 *Simpsons* episode "Worst Episode Ever," they find Comic Book Guy's secret collection of bootleg videocassettes, including the "good version" of *The Godfather Part III*, a secret plan to use Springfield as a nuclear testing range, and a tape labeled "Mister Rogers Drunk." We only hear the slurred audio: "Well, whaddya mean I can't take off my sweater? I'm *hot*!"

Fred Rogers had to live with comedians parodying him, not just once or twice, but over and over for most of his life. It was an unhappy echo of the childhood days when other kids taunted him and called him "Fat Freddy." He admitted, "It hurts me when people make fun of me, because that's who I am. The ones who do the grossest parodies really do exaggerate the way I talk."

As ever, he was able to put aside his own feelings if he could minister to other people. "There are adults who are terribly threatened by my manner, because there's something within them" that was terrified of him, Mister Rogers analyzed. "I may evoke something within them that's very tender that they never knew about and that may be very frightening to them. I think that people who put me down and feel they cannot stand that presentation of gentle masculinity have not dealt with that within themselves."

The most extreme version of that syndrome might have been Jonathan Davis, lead singer of the nu-metal band Korn, who on his song "Mr. Rogers" explicitly raged at Fred Rogers, blaming him for teaching him to be vulnerable: "Fred, you told me everybody was my neighbor / They took advantage of me, you let them take turns hitting me." It's a perverse answer song to "What Do You Do with the Mad That You Feel?": apparently, you record a loud rock track.

In his early stand-up comedy (recorded on his debut live album *Reality . . . What a Concept*), Robin Williams did an extended parody of *Mister Rogers' Neighborhood*, imagining the host getting stoned and cosmic. "Let's put Mr. Hamster in the microwave," he said in an imitation of Mister Rogers' voice. "Can you say 'severe radiation'?" Which he quickly followed with "Can you say 'entropy'? Nice try."

The phrase "Can you say" is one of the two cornerstones of a Fred Rogers impression; the other one is a red cardigan sweater. Although Mister Rogers wore a zip-up sweater on almost every show, he owned cardigans in a rainbow of colors and rotated through his collection regularly. A harvest-gold sweater went out of favor after 1989 (maybe it fell victim to moths?) while a neon-blue cardigan appeared exactly once. But crunching the data from the final twenty-three years of the *Neighborhood* (all the shows after he came back from his three-year hiatus), you learn that (1) the palette of Mister Rogers' sweaters shifted to "darker, more saturated tones" over the years; and (2) although the frequency of the red sweater gradually increased, Mister Rogers' favorite color for sweaters was actually green, by a decisive margin of seventy-four to fifty-four. (Since he was red-green color-blind, this all likely

reflects the preferences of his production staff rather than
Mister Rogers himself.)

And "Can you say"? In the popular imagination, it's Mister
Rogers' trademark phrase, the constant encouraging drumbeat of the show. In a *Bloom County* comic strip, Opus the penguin is watching the *Neighborhood* on TV, when the host asks,
"Can you say 'Mister Rogers should be paid more money'?"

Opus dutifully repeats, "Mister Rogers should—" but the
TV interrupts him, asking "Can you write it on a postcard?"

Fred objected, "Do you know that, as far as I can remember, there has *never* been a time on our program that I have said
'Can you say'?"

It turns out that this is almost true. A few times, he said
versions of the phrase: for example, in 1970, he said "Could
you say that? 'Pentagon.'" But it happened, on average, every
twenty years or so. Its popularity as a catchphrase in imitations
of the *Neighborhood* means that many Mister Rogers impressions are based on other impressions, not on actually watching
the show. "Can you say" appears to originate with Christopher
Guest, who did two sketches as "Mr. Roberts" on the 1977 National Lampoon comedy album *That's Not Funny, That's Sick*—
one of which featured him interviewing a jazz bassist played
by Bill Murray.

Close observation of Mister Rogers, however, provided the
secret DNA for a different impression: Dana Carvey as George
H. W. Bush, the forty-first president of the United States, on
Saturday Night Live. "The way to do the president is to start out
with Mister Rogers," Carvey explained in 1992. "Then you add
a little John Wayne . . . you put 'em together, you've got George
Herbert Walker Bush."

One of the most frequent parodists of Mister Rogers was Johnny Carson, in an extended series of sketches on *The Tonight Show*. Sometimes Carson would play Mister Rogers as a man with secret adult habits, like a fridge full of liquor; sometimes he would render him in "Mister Codger's Neighborhood," finding a dead bird and asking the audience "When is Mr. Parrot like Mr. Froggy, children? When he croaks"; sometimes he would mash him up with other celebrities, with results like "Mister Rambo's Neighborhood."

"I've told Johnny that I like humor as much as anybody," Fred said. "But what concerns me is that the takeoffs make me seem so wimpy! I hope it doesn't communicate that Mister Rogers is just somebody to be made fun of. Only people who take the time to see our work can begin to understand the depth of it."

Mister Rogers, a regular guest on *The Tonight Show*, said that during one appearance, Carson told him, "You know, Fred, we wouldn't do these parodies if we didn't like you."

"At first, I didn't understand what he meant," Fred said, baffled as to why somebody's words wouldn't match their deeds. Carson may have been genuinely fond of Fred Rogers; it seems equally likely that he was trying to assuage a guest.

Also frequently parodying Mister Rogers was Harvey Korman on *The Carol Burnett Show*. As Rita Moreno remembered it, "Harvey Korman many times made fun of him, and I remember thinking, 'What a stupid man. How ignorant this is.' One time when Fred was on *The Tonight Show*, guess who was also a guest star? And Harvey Korman was a little embarrassed. This is how I remember it: Korman was somewhat apologetic, and said, 'I was just kidding, that's what I do.' And you know what

Fred did? Fred said, 'Yes, but it was very hurtful.' He said it in the nicest and kindest way—but he was saying you shouldn't have done that, on television, so a million people could watch and hear it. I thought, 'This is a person who knows who he is, who knows that he has value, no matter what some asshole comic actor says.' I was so happy, because I used to hate those Fred Rogers jokes—I always said to myself, 'Listen, you jerk, this show is not for you; this show is for little children. Even though you are a child—[and] in your case, that's a problem!'"

Once in a while, Mister Rogers would take action to stop a parody. He explained, "There have been people on local stations that have gotten dressed up like me with the sneakers and the sweater and talked like me and said some outrageous things in daytime television. And they just thought they were being funny. But one, for instance, said, 'Now, children, get your mother's hair spray and your daddy's cigarette lighter, and press the buttons together, and you'll have a blowtorch.'" Fred Rogers could live with mockery, but he couldn't abide the possibility that children were being put in danger. He said, "We called the station and they put a stop to it."

Also intolerable to him: exploiting the trust that children had in him, which he regarded as a sacred bond, for mercenary purposes. He wouldn't do ads—and he wouldn't even allow commercials for *Neighborhood* toys to be aimed at children. That's why he didn't expect Burger King to release a commercial featuring "Mister Rodney" in 1989, mimicking him closely enough that it freaked out people who knew him well. (Mister Rodney wore a powder-blue sweater, not red, but his thirty-second pitch began with "Hi, neighbor" and did include the spurious catchphrase "Can you say?") Mister Rogers would have been dismayed by his image being used to sell anything, but as a longtime vegetarian, it particularly rankled him that people thought he was touting the virtues of flame-broiled hamburgers.

When Fred found out about the commercial, he promptly convened a rare press conference, making it clear that he had not consented to Burger King hijacking his likeness and his reputation. But he didn't sue—instead, he called up Don Dempsey, the senior vice president for marketing at Burger King, the man ultimately responsible for the ad.

Fred was calm and polite on the phone, even friendly. He asked Dempsey if he was a father; when the answer was yes, he asked if Dempsey's children understood what he did for a living.

Then (according to Eliot Daley, a colleague of Fred's) he said, "Well, that's wonderful. It must feel great to have them know and appreciate and be proud of what you do." Fred continued, "What do you think it would be like if they misunderstood what you do? Actually, if they thought that what you do was something bad, or you know, harmful to people, or the food that you were selling them was not good for them? And if they lost respect for what you do?"

Fred didn't threaten Burger King—he didn't need to. Relying on Don Dempsey's better angels and his own unshakable moral code was sufficient. "If this offends you personally, we will pull the commercials as quickly as we can," the executive told him. Burger King yanked the commercials off the air— they had spent $150,000 on the spot and aired it for just one week.

"Mister Rogers is one guy you don't want to mess with, as

beloved as he is," Burger King spokesman John Weir said. "So that particular commercial goes on the shelf. Hopefully, we now have peace in the neighborhood."

The most famous imitator of Fred Rogers was Eddie Murphy, who did nine installments of "Mister Robinson's Neighborhood" on *Saturday Night Live,* starting in February 1981. Mister Robinson was a small-time crook living in a tenement with peeling paint on the walls; he would enter his apartment singing "Won't You Be My Neighbor?" and change into a canary-yellow cardigan, as the lyrics shifted to something like "I've always wanted to live in a house like yours, my friend / Maybe when there's nobody home, I'll break in."

This character was a star-making role for Eddie Murphy. In *SNL*'s famously difficult fifth season, Murphy stood out because he had the confidence to look straight into the camera and speak directly with the viewers, forging the same intimate bond with teenagers staying up late on a Saturday night that Mister Rogers had with preschoolers in the daylight.

Admittedly, the subject matter was somewhat different: Mister Robinson talked about stealing an old lady's groceries or swindling kids by selling them a "Cabbage Patch Doll" (a head of cabbage impaled on the body of a doll). The role flirted with racial stereotypes, but as played by Murphy, it wasn't a ghetto caricature. Mister Robinson was sly and smart and charming, with an arrogance that was leavened with flashes of vulnerability—a rough sketch of Murphy's future persona as a global superstar.

In February 1982, Mister Rogers was a guest on *Late Night with David Letterman,* during the first month of the host's thirty-three-year run on late-night TV. Fred still knew his way around 3o Rockefeller Plaza, where the show was filmed—he had spent many hours working in NBC's Studio 8H, now home to *Saturday Night Live,* so before he went on the air with Letterman, he took an elevator to *SNL*'s offices and surprised Murphy.

The actor was taken aback—it's not every day that somebody you're parodying shows up on your doorstep—but he soon recovered from his surprise, exclaiming, "Here's the real Mister Rogers!" Eddie Murphy and Fred Rogers hugged and posed for a Polaroid together.

When Mister Rogers appeared on Letterman's show that evening—he followed Andy Kaufman, and his appearance began with an outtake from the *Neighborhood* where he wrestled with a tent, utterly failing in multiple efforts to fold it up—the host asked him about Eddie Murphy's impression of him. Mister Rogers surprised viewers by pulling out the Polaroid. Speaking generally of the parodies that were everywhere, he said, "Some of them aren't very funny. But I think a lot of them are done with real kindness in their heart."

The evidence suggested that was untrue, but it wasn't just a story that Fred told himself to make the mockery sting a little less. If he said it and believed it, then maybe other people would believe it, too. And if they did, then even caricatures of him could help with his life's work: they, too, could fan the flames of kindness in other people's hearts.

Accept the changing seasons.

It begins like any other Monday: Mister Rogers enters his television home singing, puts on a light blue sweater (with buttons, no zipper), and then looks into the camera to say "I thought about you this weekend." But this episode, which aired on March 23, 1970, is one of the most remarkable installments of *Mister Rogers' Neighborhood* because of what happens next: when Mister Rogers goes to feed the fish in the tank in his kitchen, he discovers that one of them is no longer alive.

"Do you see a dead fish?" he asks the home viewer, in a steady tone. "A dead fish would be one that isn't swimming or breathing or anything at all."

He scoops the small fish out with

a net and says that he's heard that sometimes a bath in salt water will revive a sick fish, but even after immersion in a tub of
salty water, the fish remains utterly still. He dries the goldfish off with a paper towel and calmly says, "I guess we better
bury it."

The set representing Mister Rogers' front yard has had
a patch of dirt installed for this episode. After the nameless
goldfish is consigned to its earthly grave, Mister Rogers delivers a riveting monologue, sharing an experience from his own
childhood in his usual calm tones:

> When I was very young, I had a dog that I loved very
> much. Her name was Mitzi. And she got to be old, and
> she died. And I was very sad when she died, because
> she and I were good pals. And when she died, I cried.
> My grandmother heard me crying, and she just put
> her arm around me, because she knew I was sad. She
> knew how much I loved that dog. And my dad said we'd
> have to bury Mitzi. And I didn't want to. I didn't want to
> bury her because I thought we'd pretend that she was
> still alive. But my dad said her body was dead and we'd
> have to bury her. So we did.

Mister Rogers walks inside, talking about the toy dog his
aunt and uncle gave him after Mitzi's death, and how he still
remembers Mitzi's prickly fur and curly tail.

In the Neighborhood of Make-Believe, Bob Dog learns that
Trolley—briefly nonresponsive—can't be dead, because machines aren't alive.

Back with Mister Rogers, he makes a grave marker and

sings a song that begins "Some things I don't understand / Some things are scary and sad."

In half an hour, Mister Rogers has led young children through a basic explanation of what death is, taught them about the grieving process, and told them that it's normal to feel sad and cry. "I really worked through it," he said of the show, saying that the memories of Mitzi still had emotional power for him, despite his calm demeanor. "I told the kids, 'And I cried.' I feel this is very helpful for them—to make them realize they are not isolated in their feelings."

As a young boy, Fred Rogers had received that same gift from his own father. "I'll never forget when Granddad Rogers died," he said. On the second floor of his grandparents' home, with his grandfather lying in state and visitors downstairs coming to pay their respects, young Fred found his father weeping. That made a big impression on the boy, and helped him many years later when his father died in turn. "I thought, Dad cried when his dad died. That certainly gave me broad license to cry when he died. And my sons saw me, and so when I die, I trust that they'll know that it's okay to cry, too."

Mister Rogers had many suggestions for parents looking to help their children cope with the death of a loved one: don't use confusing euphemisms like "going to sleep" or "taking a long journey," don't be upset if children make up games that help them process what death is, reassure them that you hope to be alive and taking care of them for a long time. But much of his advice for children coping with grief—hug them, talk to them, share quiet times together—was equally useful advice for adults, because death has a way of leveling and reducing everyone who encounters it.

Coping with the death of his brother, the journalist Tim Madigan told his friend Fred Rogers, "If this is where a good life leads, I wonder why we bother to be good."

Fred didn't argue theology or ethics with a man flattened by grief; Madigan's reaction was normal, even therapeutic. He just said, "I can understand how you might feel that way sometimes."

Fred believed that "with grief, there is inevitably some times of anger and, you know, God can take our anger." And so, even with our emotions churning and spinning like a particularly awful amusement-park ride, human beings blunder forward. Fred's advice: "We pray and continue to do our work, counting on God's grace to give each of us enough light to take the next steps of the journey."

Fred once said that "the Kingdom of God is for the brokenhearted." In other words, it's for everyone. What helped Fred through his own periods of grief and sorrow was his belief that life on earth was just a small portion of his soul's existence; he would sometimes discomfit nonbelievers by casually referring to his deceased loved ones as being in heaven.

Other times he would use heaven as a metaphor—"The connections we make in the course of a life, maybe that's what heaven is"—but he did so knowing that the power of faith was that it provided humanity with a metaphor for the divine. People wondered if his television Neighborhood, or maybe just the Neighborhood of Make-Believe, both idyllic places filled with love and light, were intended to be representations of heaven, and he said they were not.

The Neighborhood, according to Mister Rogers, was not meant to be seen as a utopia or a "Pollyannish state." He used the show to address, albeit gently, divorce, fear, and jealousy. None of that would be necessary in the afterlife as he saw it: "When I think about heaven, it is a state in which we are so greatly loved that there is no fear and doubt and disillusion and anxiety. It is where people really do look at you with the eyes of Jesus." Meaning that they see the truth about you, which for Fred was the same thing as seeing the best in you.

Fred used to say in unguarded moments that he'd be happy to die on the set of the *Neighborhood:* "I can't think of a better place to do that." That wasn't because he believed heaven was a place on earth, specifically a television studio in Pittsburgh, but because that studio was where he was most himself, surrounded by people he loved and doing the work that gave his life meaning. He fervently hoped that it also helped give meaning to the lives of the children watching—or more precisely, that it gave them the capacity to find that meaning.

Fred Rogers wanted the world to actually believe in the Golden Rule and act on it. He couldn't convert billions of minds in one broadcast, so he would have to settle for the life he had already chosen, persuading people in smaller batches—one at a time, if necessary. He didn't claim to know all the secrets of heaven, so he wanted us to do our best with this material world until we got there.

"Frankly, I think that after we die, we have this wide understanding of what's real," he said. "And we'll probably say, 'Ah, so that's what it was all about.'"

Share what you've learned. (All your life.)

The sun had set on *Mister Rogers' Neighborhood*. Fred Rogers had changed into his sweater and sneakers for the last time. The magic of reruns meant that he would keep feeding the fish, sending the trolley to the Neighborhood of Make-Believe, and telling children they were special, but he was relieved of the duty of performing these tasks for television cameras himself. Even in his seventies, however, Mister Rogers wasn't done illuminating the world.

He kept up a regular schedule of speeches, addressing graduating classes and charitable organizations. He no longer spoke directly to children; now he was making one last visit with adults who had been his television neighbors twenty or thirty years earlier, reminding them of the values and les-

sons of his Neighborhood. If he could hold their attention for just half an hour—the length of one of his episodes—then he could provide counterprogramming for a world full of chaos and irony and channel-flipping.

Fred Rogers gave his final public address as the keynote speaker for the seventeenth GCYF Annual Conference. "GCYF" stood for Grantmakers for Children, Youth, and Families, meaning that he was addressing a room filled with kindred spirits: fund-raisers for children's charities. The date was October 9, 2003; the location was Houston, Texas; the weather outside was muggy.

Fred didn't know he was giving his last speech—but every time he tried to change the world for the better, even a little bit, he summed up his legacy. Preparing this particular speech, Fred reviewed an address he had given in Pittsburgh four months earlier. The text of that speech was printed in bold capital letters in a narrow bar, looking like copy for a teleprompter. He marked up that text, modifying and updating it.

If you read the rough draft, annotated in Fred's looping handwriting, you can see his attention to detail and his careful editorial eye. He corrected spelling mistakes, he eliminated redundant passages, and he smoothed out awkward phrases. In a passage about a child getting sponsors for a charity walk, for example, "Her friends and family members pledged so much money a mile" became "pledged a certain amount of money per mile." It was a small improvement, but it demonstrated the care that he brought to scripts for his program, believing that his audience—whether they were adults or children—deserved his best effort to communicate as clearly as he could.

The child in that charity-walk anecdote, Julia Petruska,

was the daughter of Marge Petruska, a director at the Heinz Endowments. Years later, Marge remembered that soon after she adopted Julia—"A scrawny, wide-eyed five-year-old from an orphanage in St. Petersburg, Russia"—they attended a brunch where Fred was also a guest. Julia, who then knew only a few words of English, entertained herself by playing with the host's dogs. That lasted until Fred spotted her sitting by herself.

"He is always drawn to the ones who aren't fitting in," Marge said. Fred got down on his knees so Julia would be taller than him, and started talking with her and singing to her. When he got a passionate Russian monologue in return, he listened carefully, although he didn't speak the language. He then led Julia to the piano, finding another way to communicate with her.

Mister Rogers didn't tell Marge's story in Houston, because he didn't make himself the center of his own speech. When he spoke with audiences, he wanted them to consider the larger world. In fact, he shared just one anecdote about his own philanthropy: on the thirtieth anniversary of *Mister Rogers' Neighborhood,* his production company eschewed lavish celebrations of the longest-running show on public television, instead doing a "Neighborhood Sweater Drive," collecting more than one million sweaters all over the country and distributing them to the needy.

In this he was following the example of his mother, who during World War II, led a volunteer group that made sweaters and socks and surgical dressings for American soldiers. To his mind, her efforts on behalf of the troops and the time she spent knitting sweaters for her own family came from the same impulse—the satisfaction of helping other people.

In Houston, he showed a clip of his visit to a farm in upstate New York called Green Chimneys, founded by the doctor Sam Ross, that was a hospice not just for ailing animals but for young people in need: "They came to help care for the animals and eventually to allow the animals and Dr. Ross' professional team to care for them." And just as ministering to the animals helped the children heal themselves, ministering to the children enriched the adults at Green Chimneys. One staff member told Mister Rogers, "The children have reinforced for me that happiness is not going out and making a million dollars. But happiness is giving. The kids have given me a tremendous feeling of self-worth."

Telling the story of a woman he had never met—Zhang Shuqin, who dedicated herself to caring for the children of prisoners in China—he cited the Robert Frost dictum that his poems started as "a lump in the throat." Fred believed that charity came from that same lump in the throat and wanted to inspire his listeners to acts of generosity: not everybody would start orphanages and animal refuges, but everybody could help. Mister Rogers declared, "I think that the saddest person anywhere is the person who feels that he or she doesn't have anything of value (inside) to give."

The part of the speech that Fred wrestled with the most was his account of a trip he took to Scotland only a couple of weeks earlier. His handwritten draft on a legal pad was full of false starts, crossed-out text, and other revisions. Part of that was the typical writer's agony of bringing a paragraph to life so that it doesn't read like it has a bucket on its head as it blunders around and bumps into the metaphorical furniture. A larger issue was finding some way to make sense of news reports he had seen on his trip saying that one in six teenagers in Scotland were joining vigilante gangs, and to find a way to incorporate this information into his philosophy, let alone draw an instructive moral from it. His answer, as it so often was in times of bad news: look for the helpers.

Mister Rogers saw an interview with a child advocate in Scotland who ran a group home for teenagers, providing an alternative to prison. He remembered, "She talked about them with such compassion and said how convinced she was that underneath their hard exteriors were frightened kids who longed to be loved."

Then Mister Rogers turned to a story about a one-hundred-yard dash event at the Special Olympics in Seattle. When one boy stumbled and hurt his knee, the other contestants turned around and ran back to him. A girl with Down syndrome comforted him with a kiss; then, all nine racers linked arms and walked across the finish line together.

The truth is that the incident happened at a track meet in Spokane, Washington, in 1976, and while most of the runners continued to the finish line, one or two did go back for their fallen comrade and they completed the race together. The story likely arrived in Mister Rogers' email inbox in its exaggerated version and he believed it because he very much wanted to believe that he lived in a world where such acts of spontaneous kindness could happen.

The thing is, he did live in that world. Even before the Internet anonymously punched up the story, the essence was true, and it was a modern-day version of the Good Samaritan parable. An injured athlete found that at least one of his competitors transformed themselves into a partner. It wasn't all eight runners—but one was enough.

Mister Rogers built his life around the notion that human connection would lead to understanding, and from there to kindness and generosity. In Texas, at that last speech, he showed a video clip of one of his favorite moments of connection on the *Neighborhood*, when ten-year-old Jeff Erlanger was a guest in 1981.

Erlanger, who had spent half his life in a wheelchair, had first met Mister Rogers when he was five, just before he had surgery to fuse his spine. His parents offered to take him to Disneyland, but he said he'd rather meet Mister Rogers—which he did, when his television friend came to Milwaukee to visit the local PBS affiliate.

Five years later, *Mister Rogers' Neighborhood* was doing a week of shows on machines, both mechanical and electric. Mister Rogers decided that he wanted to feature a child in a wheelchair and that it had to be Jeff Erlanger, despite his staff's protests that there were Pittsburgh kids who fit the bill and there was no need to fly anyone in from Wisconsin. But Mister Rogers insisted and his staff tracked down the family. Before they went on the air, Mister Rogers reminded Erlanger how much he liked him, told him that they might sing a song together, and asked him not to use too many big words.

"This is my friend, Jeff Erlanger," Mister Rogers told viewers. "He's one of my neighbors here, and I asked him if he would come by today because I wanted you to meet him, and I wanted you to see his electric wheelchair." Erlanger showed off that machinery, and with gentle questioning from Mister Rogers, explained why he was in a wheelchair (a spinal tumor), named the doctors who helped with his health issues like autonomic dysreflexia (so much for avoiding big words), and the complexity of his life ("You have a lot of things happening to you most of the time when you're handicapped . . . and sometimes that happens when you're not handicapped"). And then Mister Rogers and Jeff Erlanger sang "It's You I Like" as a duet—the affection they had for each other obvious to all visitors.

The episode that resulted from this encounter wasn't just powerful television—it changed people's lives. Mister Rogers was showing children how to be accepting of the differently abled. As he once said, "When we see someone who looks or behaves differently from what's familiar to us, it's possible to feel a little shy, scared, curious, or awkward. I know how much I've struggled to look with my heart and not just my eyes when I see someone who is obviously different from me. If adults have such a challenge, imagine what a challenge that can be for children."

Fred Rogers meeting Jeff Erlanger became one of the most famous, powerful sequences in *Neighborhood* history, one he shared with audiences many times over the years. Talking about people watching that clip, a Family Communications employee said, "Everybody always cries. I've seen it over and over, and *I* always cry. When you're there in the hall, though, you can see the power of it. Everybody's face suddenly goes all soft. It's almost like you're watching people through a special lens."

In 1999, almost two decades after Jeff Erlanger visited the Neighborhood, Mister Rogers was inducted into the Television Hall of Fame, alongside a half dozen other luminaries, including executive Fred Silverman, comedian Carl Reiner, and *Saturday Night Live* producer Lorne Michaels.

Mister Rogers showed the Houston audience a clip from the Hall of Fame ceremony, which had happened in a North Hollywood theater packed with showbiz luminaries: twenty-eight-year-old Jeff Erlanger, clad in a tuxedo, rolls onto the stage to honor Mister Rogers. Mouth gaping in surprise, Mister Rogers jumps out of his seat and climbs onto the stage to give Erlanger a hug.

When he gave his Hall of Fame acceptance speech, Mister Rogers made a request that was important to him, one that he repeated in Houston. He wanted his listeners to think about the people who had helped them succeed. "Who are the people who have helped you become who you are today?" he asked. "Nobody gets to be a human adult without the investment of others all along the way. I'd like to give you a minute in the middle of this meeting to think of those who have trusted you and guided you and loved you into being . . . a minute of grateful silence."

As usual, Mister Rogers told his audience that he would watch the time. A minute was enough time for silence to settle in, for the adults to contemplate all the people they owed so much for having shepherded them through childhood. Some of them may even have considered their debt to Fred Rogers.

At the end of the minute, he told his listeners, "Whomever you've been thinking about, whether they're here today, or far away, or even in heaven, imagine how grateful they would be to know how you feel about them here and now." The ability to help other people was a gift; so was memory; so was gratitude.

"The generous human spirit is exceedingly powerful," Mister Rogers reminded his listeners. As he concluded his remarks, Mister Rogers urged everyone in the room to give generously, to receive graciously, and to exercise their strength through wisdom.

Fred Rogers had a final chance to sum up his approach to life, to explain how he had tried to spend the seventy-four years he had been given. He had said it before, many times in many different ways, but he had never been afraid of repeating himself. He would keep saying it until you were ready to listen. "You can't satisfy all the desires of those who ask, but you can translate some of the care you have inside of yourselves to action on the outside," he told everyone one last time. "And that's what really matters."

Acknowledgments

Thank you, Fred McFeely Rogers, for helping me grow up with such gentle care, the way you helped so many people. And thank you for the way you lived your life, which has given me inspiration again now that I'm an adult.

Thank you to Carrie Thornton, who edited this book with her usual panache. Thank you to all her kick-ass colleagues at Dey Street Books, including Tatiana Dubin, Paula Szafranski, Greg Villepique, Andrea Molitor, Stephanie Vallejo, Danielle Bartlett, Kell Wilson, and Andrea Peabbles.

Many thanks to my agent Daniel Greenberg and all his comrades at the Levine-Greenberg-Rostan agency who staunchly look after my interests, especially Tim Wojcik and Miek Coccia.

Thank you to the brilliant illustrator R. Sikoryak; this is our third collaboration (the other two being *The Tao of Bill Murray* and *The World According to Tom Hanks*) and he constantly astonishes me with his artistic gifts and his easygoing genius. Go check out all his other books and comics. (And he would like to thank his wife, Kriota Willberg.)

Thanks to Emily Uhrin at the Fred Rogers Center in Latrobe, Pennsylvania, for her assistance with their archives. For advice and aid, many thanks to Temilade Adejumo, Alan Bunce, Stephanie Cozart Burton, Liz Carlson, Carole D'Agostino, Stephanie Dempsey, Tim Ferrin, Danielle Fuerth, Paul Goldberg, LJ Gysel, Thane Gysel, Dean Jordan, Judy Katz, Nina Kiersted, Kevin Leonard, Jeff Malmberg, Jen McGivney, Monica Morita, Bernadelle Richter, and Basil Twist.

Thanks to all my neighbors in all my neighborhoods, especially the awe-inspiring Rob Sheffield for his essential feedback on an early version of this manuscript, which made the book better in a thousand ways. Thanks to my dear friend Jeff Jackson, whose deep knowledge of both Andy Warhol and George Romero was incredibly helpful. Thanks to Bill Tipper and Steve Crystal for long-distance advice and encouragement, and to James Hannaham (my one-time Fred Rogers memorial-service coconspirator) for being his excellent self. And this book wouldn't exist without the well-timed hospitality and generosity of Chuck Barger—my profound thanks to him.

Jen Sudul Edwards, the woman I love, is a brilliant, generous dynamo of a human being who's an inspiration to just about everybody she crosses paths with—and that's a lot of people—but I'm the one who's lucky enough to be married to her.

This book is dedicated to my two wonderful sons, Dashiell and Strummer, who fill my life with adventure and dancing and birds. Dashiell asked for me to dedicate a book to him, which I was extremely happy to do—although I know he would really have preferred that it was about Samuel L. Jackson.

And my thanks to you, for reading this book. Like Mister Rogers, I like you just the way you are.

Sources

I am indebted to the work of many scholars, journalists, and fans of Mister Rogers who came before me. A detailed list of sources and endnotes can be found on my website at https://rulefortytwo.com/books/kindness-and-wonder-sources/. But I particularly thank my interview subjects Ben Adelman, Hilary Appelman, John Bell, Barbara Bingham, Bob Brown, LeVar Burton, Tony Cartledge, Holly Cornwell, Nancy Donahue, Pat Donahue, I-Jen Fang, Arthur Greenwald, Kay Griffith, Ella Jenkins, Doris Jones, Jessica Bass Kirk, Skip LaPlante, Spencer Lott, Rita Moreno, Kweilin Nassar, Saihou Omar Njie, Bill Nye, Jay O'Callahan, Walt Seng, Lynn Swann, and Nick Tallo, all of whom were generous enough to share their time and memories with me. If you're interested in reading more about Mister Rogers, I found the following books and articles particularly illuminating:

Robert King Clark, "Misterogers' Neighborhood: A Historical and Descriptive Analysis," Ohio State University dissertation, 1971.

Sally Ann Flecker, "When Fred Met Margaret," *Pittmed*, Winter 2014.

Amy Hollingsworth, *The Simple Faith of Mister Rogers: Spiritual Insights from the World's Most Beloved Neighbor*, Thomas Nelson, 2005.

Tom Junod, "Can You Say . . . Hero?," *Esquire*, November 1998.

John Kenyon, "A Conversation with Fred Rogers," *Christian Herald*, March 1980.

Margaret Mary Kimmel, Ph.D., and Mark Collins, *The Wonder of It All: Fred Rogers and the Story of an Icon*, Fred Rogers Center, September 2008.

Maxwell King, *The Good Neighbor: The Life and Work of Fred Rogers*, Abrams, 2018.

Michael G. Long, *Peaceful Neighbor: Discovering the Countercultural Mister Rogers*, Westminster John Knox, 2015.

Fred Rogers, *Dear Mister Rogers: Does It Ever Rain in Your Neighborhood?*, Penguin, 1996.

Fred Rogers, *The World According to Mister Rogers: Important Things to Remember*, 2003. Reprint, Hachette Books, 2014.

Fred Rogers, *Life's Journeys According to Fred Rogers: Things to Remember Along the Way*, 2005. Reprint, Hachette Books, 2014.

John Sedgwick, "Who the Devil Is Fred Rogers?," *Wigwag*, November 1989.

"Door Interview: Mr. Fred Rogers," *The Wittenburg Door*, Number 37, June-July 1977.

I can also wholeheartedly recommend the exhaustive
website theneighborhoodarchive.com (a labor of love by
Spencer Fruhling), the documentary *Mister Rogers & Me* (directed by the brothers Benjamin Wagner and Christofer Wagner), the interviews of Fred Rogers and Josie Carey conducted
by Karen Herman and hosted on the Archive of American
Television website, and, of course, the documentary *Won't You
Be My Neighbor?* (directed by the gracious and talented Mor-
gan Neville, who has been responsible for a great number of
snappy new days).

Index